AF399700

Maher Asaad Baker

Echoes of Heritage

ISBN Softcover: 978-3-384-20870-5

ISBN Hardback: 978-3-384-20871-2

ISBN E-Book: 978-3-384-20872-9

ISBN Large print: 978-3-384-20873-6

CONTENTS

INTRODUCTION

The folk music of Portugal tells a story as deep and enduring as the Earth itself. Passed down through uncounted generations, these melodies carry ancestral memories imprinted in lyrics and rhythm. Their hidden messages quietly shaped the Portuguese soul over centuries, instilling virtues of rootedness, community, and reverence for life's beauty in hardship.

Today, as modernity rends old ways, folk music's influence waxeth subtle yet remaineth potent. Its allure draweth some to rediscover origins in song. For music hath power to reawaken what sleeps in blood and soil, stirring nostalgia for mysteries of whence we came.

Traditional folk ballads unfold simple tales through repetition and refrain. Often concerning trials of love or labor, their lyrics spring from the daily experiences of an agrarian people. Melodies follow fado's melancholic mood yet hold surprise notes of joy in suffering's fleeting beauty. Instrumentation maintains intimacy through lone guitar or accordion. Performed around hearthstones or in taverns, their mode is communal sharing more than show.

Two elements endure across variations - querencia da terrinha and saudade. Terrinha signifies attachment to the homeland, its familiar landscapes, and its way of life. Saudade expresses a longing for persons and times past, a bittersweet nostalgia recognizing life's transience. Together they form folk music's emotional core, a bittersweet solace found in celebrating what time threatens to erase. Their undercurrents of attachment and impermanence speak to anxieties of modern drift, a longing to anchor in nature's steady rhythms.

Portugal's musical roots intertwine with the history of cultural struggle. After Reconquista's vict'ry o'er Moorish rule, folkways consoled peasants toiling in the feudal system's shadow. Hymns joined fado's refrains in fields and along pilgrimage routes. Their mingled strains breathed resilience into daily toil, portraying hardship as an opportunity to prove virtue. Music accompanied rites making sacred the cycles life demands, finding transcendence through honest labor.

This fostered an ethos valuing dutiful acceptance of rebellious desire. Songs retold saints' trials, affirming life's fleeting comforts but eternal rewards in the afterlife. Their messages aligned with Christian stoicism, cultivating gratitude for simple gifts like love, harvest, or healing wounds. This fortified the folk against fortune's blows, seeing providence in privations. Their faith-filled music calmed storms within by reference to a greater purpose beyond immediate want or woe.

Under folk music's surface simplicity flow deeper currents, messages absorbed since youth imprinting character. Recurrent themes of rootedness, fellowship, and perseverance instilled collective habits that secured culture for ages. Their subtle moral instruction aligned individuals with communitarian purpose, where each plays a vital role in supporting the whole. Songs passed down familial and regional identities, cultivating pride in heritage while

honoring the continuity of life through children.

Moreover, the songs remind us that existence entwines our fates, for good or ill, in relations hard to sever. This inspires humility before life's grandeur and our smallness within it, but also compassion recognizing shared frailty. Their evocation of saudade denotes our ephemeral yet enduring connections, how souls depart yet remain through love's residue in lives touched. In this way, folk music transmits civilization's accumulated kindness across the generations.

The role of music in Portuguese culture runs as deep as the roots of its land. Over centuries,

---

melodies took form reflecting the soul of a people shaped by remoteness and struggle under changeable skies. Songs stitched together isolated communities, easing hardship through communal spirit. Their influence endured as changing times tested traditions, imparting virtues that secured national character in diversity.

Even amid modern currents eroding uniqueness, the music maintains powerful significance. Its lessons persist unconsciously through generations, instilling a resilient identity.

Portugal's isolated terrain bred self-sufficiency amongst varied regions, each cultivating niche skills and dialects. Yet folk songs spanned differences, intimating shared experiences of labor and longing. Rural melodies centered on family, faith, and frugal joys of harvest festivals. They breathed fortitude into lives daily confronting nature's changes and calamities outside control.

Through music, peasants eased toils by mirroring nature's consoling rhythms. Songs accompanied tasks from sowing to supper, making work cheerful communion. Their lyrics reminded temporary hardship's purpose in God's design, finding strength through steadfast duty rather than dissatisfaction's delusions. Ballads passed moral guidance between generations, instilling humility, community, and gratitude as a balm for fleeting troubles.

Over centuries, variants spread yet core virtues endured. Songbooks archived regional flavor while maintaining Portuguese-ness by common threads. Their heritage linked disparate pasts, cultivating nationality from diversity's seeds. Even as modernity eroded folkways, music preserved ancestral roots nourishing identity in flux. Its time-tested lessons persist unconsciously, an inheritance shaping character.

As explorers braved oceans, sailors carried rhythms evoking home amongst perils. Songs buoyed morale through homesickness and dangers, giving purpose to isolation. Their familiar comforts kindled crew solidarity in facing uncertainty. Ballads told seafaring narratives, honoring daring that expanded borders. Later, immigrants kept cultural ties through tunes in new lands, adapting melodies to life's changing courses.

Maritime adventures spawned global trade, spreading Portuguese cultural flavor. Music accompanied evangelism through Fado's migration. Its melancholy genre evolved with empire yet retained emotional essence, voicing longing for loved ones across seas. Songs traversed frontiers, spreading national character abroad even as borders stretched. Their common melodies intimated shared heritage wherever strangers met with familiar phrases.

Music accompanied revolutionary acts establishing Portugal's role in a changing world. Its rhythms accompanied conquest, but also cultural encounters breeding diversity. Songs maintained identity amid flux, consoling through change just as folks had weathered chance's turns for ages. Melodies accompanied soldiers and colonists spreading influence, outpacing geography as cultural ambassadors. Their ties of the song linked Portuguese everywhere to origins, wherever life's currents bore them.

Instruments carry cultural fingerprints as distinctive as dialects. Through unique timbres, sounds shaped Portugal's musical signature abroad. The Portuguese guitar lent plaintive tones to melancholy fado, giving voice to lives between hope and hardship. Its soft notes impart a window into the soul of a people accustomed to finding poignant beauty even in suffering.

Other strings like the violin and Portuguese

mandolin joined rural merriment, filling festivals with lively steps. Percussion kept complex rhythms for dances recalling fertility rites, blending pagan roots with Catholic pageantry. Accordions and bagpipes in northern regions spoke of Celtic blood mingled over invasions. Brass band parades fostered civic solidarity in changing times.

Each sound imparted the region's ethos across frontiers. Their timbres epitomized national identity beyond words, a musical passport conveying essence abroad. Flavors mingled through immigration, adapting overseas yet retaining hints of origins. Just as dialects evolved from Rome and Moors, instruments blended influences across the ages. Today harmonies echo Portugal's vivacity just as its melancholic nostalgia, recalling a tale of perseverance through diversity.

Though threatened by commercial standardization, folkways persist through contemporary strains celebrating cultural patrimony. Emerging genres fuse tradition with modern allure, reaching new audiences without compromising heritage. Artists revive old sounds whilst adding innovation, ensuring music's relevance amid global flows.

Fado endures worldwide popularity through

fresh narratives updating its meaning. New interpreters convey life's mixtures of hope and heartbreak through traditional modes. Jazz and other fusion genres infuse old refrains with renewed vigor, preserving cultural memory through new expression. Music survives by adapting without betraying virtues instilled over eras. Contemporary artists renew tradition's lessons to contemporary struggles.

Festivals amplify folkways' communal spirit countrywide, drawing outsiders into intimacy. Events showcase regional flavors, cultivating citizens' pride in diversity. Music joins mass movements celebrating nationality amid shifting times. Its role expands publicly while privately nurturing roots of identity handed down through generations. Songs maintain continuity of cultural story when other ties weaken, ensuring music remains the soul of the nation.

Through centuries, music evolved with Portugal yet retained essential character. Its role extends beyond entertainment into cultural embodiment, a subtle shaper of nationhood imprinting virtues through simplicity. Melodies accompanied every phase of Portugal's destiny, imparting fortitude through upheavals altering landscape and people.

Song preserved traits of perseverance,

community, and resourcefulness nurtured by remoteness. Its traditional forms and innovative strains convey meaning to modern lives confronting shifting global currents. Even as ways change, the music maintains relevance by adaptably imparting ancestral wisdom. Its sounds distill Portugal's essence across the generations, ensuring identity endures where other ties weaken. In this way, music fulfills its role as the soul of the people, a cultural spirit breathing life into the Portuguese story.

A HISTORICAL PRELUDE

Portugal's musical landscape is a tapestry of rich cultural traditions, weaving together the diverse influences that have shaped the nation's sonic identity over the centuries. From the soulful strains of fado to the infectious rhythms of traditional folk music, the origins of Portuguese music are a captivating and multifaceted story, reflecting the country's unique historical journey.

Portugal's strategic location on the Iberian Peninsula, with its Atlantic coastline and proximity to the Mediterranean, has played a pivotal role in shaping the evolution of its music. The country's geographical position has facilitated the influx of diverse cultural influences, as maritime trade routes and migratory patterns have brought a tapestry of musical traditions to its shores.

The rugged terrain and varied climate of Portugal have also contributed to the development of distinct regional musical styles. In the north, the mountainous regions have given rise to a rich tapestry of folk music, characterized by the use of traditional instruments such as the cavaquinho and the viola braguesa. The southern regions, with their milder climate and proximity to the sea, have fostered the emergence of styles like fado, which draw inspiration from the melancholic saudade.

Portugal's musical heritage is a testament to the nation's long history of cultural exchange and intermingling. The country's strategic location has made it a hub for cross-cultural interactions, with successive waves of invaders, traders, and settlers leaving indelible marks on the musical landscape.

The Moorish occupation of the Iberian Peninsula, for instance, introduced the influence of Arabic music, with its distinctive modes, rhythms, and instrumentation. This can be heard in the haunting melodies and intricate ornamentations of certain Portuguese musical traditions. Similarly, the Jewish diaspora, which found refuge in Portugal, contributed to the development of musical styles that incorporated elements of Sephardic and Ladino traditions.

The Age of Discoveries, which saw Portuguese explorers traversing the globe, also brought an influx of musical influences from Africa, Asia, and the Americas. The rhythmic patterns and melodic sensibilities of these distant lands were incorporated into the evolving Portuguese musical canon, creating a rich tapestry of hybridized styles.

No exploration of Portuguese music would be complete without delving into the enduring legacy of fado, a quintessential musical genre that has become deeply intertwined with the nation's cultural identity. Fado, with its soulful melodies and evocative lyrics, is often described as the "music of the soul," capturing the essence of the Portuguese experience.

The origins of fado can be traced back to the early 19th century when it emerged as a reflection of the urban working-class experience in Lisbon. Drawing on a blend of African, Brazilian, and European influences, fado initially found its footing in the taverns and back alleys of the city, before gradually gaining widespread recognition and evolving into a revered art form.

The lyrical content of fado often grapples with themes of longing, loss, and the human condition, offering a poignant commentary on the complexities of life. The genre's distinctive sound, characterized by the melancholic strains of the Portuguese guitar and the emotive vocals of its practitioners, has captivated audiences both within and beyond Portugal's borders.

Alongside the enduring legacy of fado, Portugal's rich tapestry of traditional folk music has played a vital role in shaping the nation's musical identity. From the northern regions to the southern coastlines, the country boasts a diverse array of regional styles, each with its own unique instrumentation, rhythmic patterns, and cultural significance.

In the Minho region, for instance, the traditional music is characterized by the use of the cavaquinho, a small four-stringed guitar that is often accompanied by the concertina and the tambourine. These lively, rhythmic melodies are often associated with celebrations and social gatherings, reflecting the vibrant community spirit of the local population.

In the Alentejo region, the traditional music is marked by the haunting, modal melodies of the viola campaniça, a distinctive guitar-like instrument that has become a symbol of the region's rural heritage. The melancholic and introspective nature of these musical traditions is often linked to the region's history of agricultural labor and the challenges of rural life.

The deep-rooted influence of religious traditions has also left an indelible mark on the evolution of Portuguese music. The country's Catholic heritage, in particular, has been a significant shaping force, with the music of the church and the celebration of religious festivals playing a crucial role in the development of various musical styles.

The rich liturgical music of the Catholic Church, with its intricate polyphonic structures and soaring choral arrangements, has been a significant source of inspiration for Portuguese composers throughout history. The influence of Gregorian chants and the music of the Iberian monastic tradition can be heard in the sacred repertoire of Portugal's cathedrals and churches.

Furthermore, the celebration of religious festivals, such as the Festa dos Tabuleiros in Tomar and the Procissão dos Passos in Braga, has given rise to vibrant musical traditions that intertwine devotional practices with the rhythmic energy of folk music. These celebrations, which often feature processions, chants, and the use of traditional instruments, serve as living repositories of Portugal's deep-rooted religious and cultural heritage.

While Portugal's musical identity is often

associated with its rich folk traditions and the enduring legacy of fado, the country has also made significant contributions to the realm of classical and art music. The development of Portuguese classical music has been shaped by the country's cultural exchanges with its European neighbors, as well as the creative vision of its homegrown composers.

The 18th and 19th centuries saw the emergence of renowned Portuguese composers, such as João Domingos Bomtempo and António Leal Moreira, who sought to establish a distinct national voice within the broader European classical tradition. These composers drew inspiration from the country's folk music, incorporating elements of traditional melodies and rhythmic patterns into their orchestral works and chamber pieces.

The 20th century witnessed a flourishing of Portuguese art music, with composers like Fernando Lopes-Graça and Joly Braga Santos pushing the boundaries of traditional forms and exploring new musical idioms. These artists sought to reconcile the country's rich musical heritage with the evolving aesthetic sensibilities of the modern era, creating a vibrant and multifaceted classical music scene.

As the 21st century unfolds, the musical

landscape of Portugal continues to evolve, with contemporary artists and musicians building upon the rich tapestry of the country's musical past. While the traditional styles of fado and folk music remain deeply revered, a new generation of musicians is experimenting with innovative approaches, blending the timeless melodies of the past with contemporary sounds and technologies.

The rise of fusion genres, such as fado-jazz and fado-electronica, has breathed new life into the country's musical heritage, appealing to younger audiences while maintaining a connection to the enduring spirit of the nation's musical identity. Additionally, the emergence of world music festivals and collaborations between Portuguese artists and their counterparts from around the globe has further enriched the nation's musical landscape, fostering a dynamic exchange of ideas and creative inspiration.

As Portugal continues to navigate the currents of cultural globalization, its musical legacy remains a testament to the resilience and adaptability of its artistic spirit. From the haunting melodies of fado to the rhythmic exuberance of traditional folk music, the origins and evolution of Portuguese music reflect the country's unique place in the world, a tapestry of timeless melodies that continue to captivate audiences both near and far.

The Iberian Peninsula, of which Portugal is an integral part, has long been a crossroads of civilizations, with the Moorish occupation of the region from the 8th to the 15th centuries leaving an indelible mark on its cultural and artistic heritage. The influence of Moorish music can be profoundly felt in the development of Portuguese music, particularly in the realm of modal structures, intricate ornamentation, and the use of specific instruments.

The Moorish musical tradition, rooted in the rich

cultural legacy of the Arab world, introduced the concept of maqamat, a system of modal scales that imbued the music with a distinct sense of tonality and emotional resonance. These modal structures, characterized by their evocative and contemplative qualities, can be heard in the haunting melodies of traditional Portuguese styles, such as the melancholic fado.

Moreover, the Moorish presence in the Iberian Peninsula led to the introduction of several musical instruments that would become integral to the Portuguese soundscape. The oud, a pear-shaped lute, and the nay, an end-blown flute, are two notable examples that found their way into the hands of Portuguese musicians, shaping the timbres and improvisational techniques that define the country's musical identity.

The intermingling of Moorish and Iberian musical traditions also gave rise to the development of new hybrid forms, such as the modhinha, a style that blended Moorish-influenced melodic structures with the lyrical sensibilities of Portuguese folk music. This cross-pollination of cultural elements created a rich tapestry of musical expression that continues to resonate in the contemporary Portuguese musical landscape.

The Age of Discoveries, a pivotal era in Portugal's history, saw the nation's explorers traversing the globe and establishing trade routes and colonial outposts across Africa, Asia, and the Americas. This far-reaching expansion had a profound impact on the country's musical evolution, as the influx of African cultural influences left an indelible mark on the Portuguese soundscape.

The rhythmic patterns and percussive elements of African music, particularly from the Lusophone (Portuguese-speaking) regions of the African continent, became deeply interwoven into the fabric of Portuguese folk and popular music. The introduction of instruments such as the djembe, the agogô, and the pandeiro infused the traditional music of Portugal with a pulsating, syncopated energy that breathed new life into the country's sonic identity.

Furthermore, the melismatic vocal styles and call-and-response structures of African musical traditions found their way into the expressive range of Portuguese singers, particularly in the realm of fado. The emotive and improvisational nature of these African-influenced vocal techniques lent an additional layer of depth and soulfulness to the quintessential Portuguese genre.

The synergy between African and Portuguese musical elements can be heard in the development of hybrid styles, such as the samba-canção, which blended the rhythmic vitality of Brazilian samba with the melancholic lyricism of fado. This cross-cultural fertilization not only enriched the musical tapestry of Portugal but also fostered a dynamic exchange of artistic ideas and creative inspiration.

As a nation situated at the westernmost edge of the Iberian Peninsula, Portugal's musical heritage has also been profoundly shaped by its close cultural and artistic ties with the broader European continent. The country's proximity to Spain and its historical connections with other European powers have facilitated the exchange of musical ideas, techniques, and aesthetic sensibilities.

The influence of European classical music, in particular, can be observed in the development of Portugal's art music traditions. Composers such as João Domingos Bomtempo and Luís de Freitas Branco, who were steeped in the European classical tradition, sought to establish a distinct national voice within the broader Western art music canon. Their compositions, infused with the rhythmic and melodic elements of Portuguese folk music, contributed to the creation of a uniquely Portuguese classical music idiom.

Furthermore, the adoption and adaptation of European instruments, such as the violin, the piano, and the classical guitar, into the Portuguese musical landscape expanded the timbral palette and expressive possibilities of the country's musicians. These instruments, combined with the technical virtuosity and compositional prowess of Portuguese artists, led to the development of a vibrant classical music scene that continues to thrive in the present day.

The influence of European folk music traditions, particularly from neighboring Spain, can also be discerned in the evolution of Portuguese folk styles. The intermingling of Iberian musical elements, such as the characteristic rhythms and modal structures, has resulted in the creation of shared musical sensibilities that transcend national boundaries, forging a sense of cultural kinship within the broader Iberian musical sphere.

The harmonious tapestry of Moorish, African, and European influences on Portuguese music has created a rich and multifaceted sonic landscape that continues to captivate audiences both within and beyond the nation's borders. These diverse cultural streams have converged, coalesced, and cross-pollinated over the centuries, giving rise to a musical identity that is at once deeply rooted in tradition and open to innovative expressions.

The enduring synergy between these cultural influences is manifested in the contemporary musical landscape of Portugal, where artists and musicians continue to explore new ways of blending the timeless melodies and rhythmic foundations of the past with modern sensibilities and experimental approaches. From the emergence of fusion genres that seamlessly integrate fado with jazz, electronic, and world music elements to the collaborative efforts between Portuguese musicians and their counterparts from across the globe, the musical heritage of Portugal remains a dynamic and ever-evolving tapestry.

As we delve into the intricate interplay of Moorish, African, and European influences on Portuguese music, we uncover a profound story of cultural exchange, artistic resilience, and the enduring power of music to transcend boundaries and forge connections. The musical legacy of Portugal stands as a testament to the nation's rich and multifaceted identity, a harmonious tapestry that continues to captivate and inspire audiences around the world.

The diverse tapestry of Portugal's traditional folk music serves as a testament to the country's rich cultural heritage, preserving the unique identities and artistic expressions of its various regions.

As the passage of time has unfolded, the traditional musical forms of Portugal have undergone a dynamic process of evolution, adapting and transforming in response to the changing tides of cultural, social, and technological influences.

The evolution of fado, the quintessential musical form of Portugal, has been a captivating journey, marked by the interplay of tradition and innovation. While the core elements of the genre – the haunting melodies, the emotive vocals, and the distinctive sound of the Portuguese guitar – have remained steadfast, fado has undergone a remarkable metamorphosis over the decades.

In the early 20th century, the emergence of renowned fado interpreters, such as Amália Rodrigues, helped to elevate the genre from its urban working-class origins to the realm of high art. These artists not only captivated audiences with their soulful performances but also expanded the expressive possibilities of fado, infusing it with a newfound sense of sophistication and artistic integrity.

As the 20th century progressed, the influence of broader musical trends and the cross-pollination of cultural elements began to shape the evolution of fado. The emergence of fusion genres, such as fado-jazz and fado-electronica, has breathed new life into the traditional form, blending its timeless melodies with contemporary sounds and technologies.

These innovative approaches have not only appealed to younger audiences but have also challenged the conventional boundaries of fado, pushing the genre to explore new creative territories while remaining firmly rooted in its rich cultural heritage.

The evolution of traditional folk music in Portugal has been a dynamic and multifaceted process, marked by the interplay of enduring traditions and the assimilation of contemporary influences.

While the core regional styles and the use of traditional instruments have remained central to the folk music landscape, the 20th and 21st centuries have witnessed a gradual transformation of these musical forms. The incorporation of modern instrumentation, such as electric guitars and synthesizers, has expanded the timbral palette of Portuguese folk music, allowing it to resonate with younger generations.

Furthermore, the emergence of fusion genres that blend traditional folk elements with contemporary musical idioms, such as world music and pop, has rejuvenated the folk music tradition, making it more accessible and appealing to broader audiences. These hybridized forms have not only preserved the essence of the traditional styles but have also forged new connections between the past and the present, ensuring the continued relevance and evolution of Portugal's folk music heritage.

The evolution of religious music in Portugal has also been a dynamic process, marked by the interplay of enduring traditions and the influence of contemporary sociocultural shifts.

While the sacred repertoire of the Catholic Church, with its rich liturgical music, has remained a constant in Portugal's musical landscape, the 20th and 21st centuries have witnessed a gradual adaptation of these forms to meet the changing needs and sensibilities of the modern era.

The introduction of vernacular languages in liturgical music, the incorporation of more contemporary musical styles and instrumentation, and the emergence of new devotional practices have all contributed to the evolution of religious music in Portugal. These adaptations have not only kept the tradition relevant but have also allowed it to resonate with a wider audience, fostering a deeper connection between the sacred and the contemporary spheres of musical expression.

Moreover, the collaboration between traditional religious music practitioners and contemporary artists has led to the creation of innovative hybrid forms that blend the timeless qualities of the sacred repertoire with fresh creative perspectives. These collaborations have not only enriched the musical tapestry of Portugal but have also served as a bridge between the enduring traditions of the past and the ever-evolving artistic sensibilities of the present.

As the tides of time have ebbed and flowed, the traditional musical forms of Portugal have demonstrated remarkable resilience, adapting and transforming to meet the demands of the contemporary era. While the essence of these enduring traditions remains steadfast, the evolution of fado, folk music, and religious music has been a captivating journey, marked by the interplay of cultural, social, and technological influences.

The legacy of Fado, with its soulful melodies and evocative lyrics, continues to captivate audiences both within and beyond Portugal's borders. The genre's ability to evolve and embrace new creative perspectives has ensured its enduring relevance, as it seamlessly blends the timeless qualities of tradition with the dynamism of the modern age.

The rich tapestry of regional folk music traditions has also demonstrated a remarkable capacity for adaptation, with the incorporation of contemporary elements breathing new life into these enduring forms. The enduring appeal of these traditional styles, coupled with their ability to forge connections with younger generations, serves as a testament to the resilience and adaptability of Portugal's musical heritage.

The evolution of religious music in Portugal, with its fusion of sacred and contemporary elements, has also played a vital role in shaping the nation's musical landscape. The ability of these traditional forms to evolve and resonate with the changing needs of the modern era underscores the enduring significance of the sacred repertoire in the cultural fabric of the country.

As we bear witness to the continued evolution of Portugal's traditional musical forms, we are reminded of the profound resilience and adaptability of the nation's artistic spirit. The enduring legacies of fado, folk music, and religious music stand as a testament to the timeless power of music to captivate, inspire, and unite audiences across generations and cultural boundaries.

The evolution of traditional musical forms in Portugal is a captivating and multifaceted story, one that reflects the enduring resilience and adaptability of the nation's artistic spirit. From the soulful strains of fado to the rhythmic exuberance of regional folk music traditions, the sonic landscape of Portugal has been shaped by the dynamic interplay of enduring traditions and the ever-changing tides of cultural, social, and technological influences.

At the heart of this evolving tapestry lie the anchors of tradition – the quintessential musical forms that have served as the foundations of Portugal's sonic identity. Fado, with its haunting melodies and emotive lyrics, has weathered the passage of time, evolving to embrace new creative perspectives while maintaining its essence. The rich tapestry of regional folk music traditions has also demonstrated a remarkable capacity for adaptation, blending the timeless qualities of the past with the dynamism of the present.

As we have delved into the metamorphosis of these traditional musical forms, we have witnessed a captivating journey marked by the interplay of cultural, social, and technological influences. The incorporation of modern instrumentation, the emergence of fusion genres, and the collaborative efforts between tradition-bearers and contemporary artists have all contributed to the dynamic evolution of Portugal's musical heritage.

The enduring legacies of fado, folk music, and religious music in Portugal stand as a testament to the timeless power of music to captivate, inspire, and unite audiences across generations and cultural boundaries. As the

---

nation's traditional musical forms continue to evolve, adapting and transforming to meet the demands of the contemporary era, they serve as a living embodiment of the resilience and adaptability of Portugal's artistic spirit.

FADO

To delve into the intricate tapestry of Portugal's musical legacy is to embark on a captivating journey through the very essence of the nation's cultural identity. At the heart of this tapestry lies the enigmatic and captivating art form known as Fado - a musical genre that has transcended the boundaries of time and space, etching its indelible mark on the hearts and souls of the Portuguese people.

Fado, in its purest form, is a reflection of the Portuguese spirit - a harmonious blend of melancholia, resilience, and an unwavering commitment to the preservation of tradition. This musical genre, which has its roots firmly planted in the cobblestone streets of Lisbon, has evolved over the centuries, adapting to the changing tides of societal and cultural shifts, yet maintaining a steadfast allegiance to its essence.

To understand the origins and evolution of Fado is to delve into the very fabric of the Portuguese national identity, a tapestry woven with threads of history, emotion, and the indomitable human spirit. It is a journey that takes us from the humble beginnings of this musical form to its ascension as a global phenomenon, captivating audiences far beyond the borders of the Iberian Peninsula.

The origins of Fado, much like the genre itself, are shrouded in a veil of mystery and speculation. While the exact moment of its inception remains elusive, scholars and historians have pieced together a narrative that offers insights into the formative years of this captivating musical form.

One school of thought suggests that the roots

of Fado can be traced back to the melancholic songs of the African slaves who were brought to Portugal during the colonial era. These soulful laments, infused with a sense of yearning and loss, are believed to have laid the foundation for the distinctive sound that would later come to define Fado.

Another perspective suggests that Fado's lineage can be found in the traditional ballads and folk songs of the Iberian Peninsula, which were deeply influenced by the cultural exchanges between Portugal, Spain, and the Moorish territories. These musical traditions, imbued with a sense of melancholy and a deep-seated connection to the land, would eventually coalesce to give birth to the unique sound of Fado.

Regardless of its precise origins, the emergence of Fado in the bustling streets of Lisbon during the late 18th and early 19th centuries is a matter of historical record. It was during this period that Fado began to take shape as a distinct musical genre, characterized by its haunting melodies, intricate guitar accompaniment, and the emotive, soulful voices of its practitioners.

As Fado began to gain recognition and

---

popularity within the cultural landscape of Portugal, a network of specialized establishments known as "Fado Houses" (Casas de Fado) emerged as the epicenters of this musical tradition. These intimate, dimly lit establishments became the sanctuaries where Fado was nurtured, celebrated, and passed down from one generation to the next.

The Fado Houses served as more than just performance venues; they were the crucibles where the essence of Fado was forged and refined. Within these hallowed walls, the greatest Fado vocalists and instrumentalists would gather, engaging in a captivating exchange of musical ideas, techniques, and

---

interpretations. The Fado Houses became the incubators of tradition, where the nuances and subtleties of this art form were meticulously preserved and honed.

Yet, the Fado Houses were not merely bastions of tradition; they were also the breeding grounds for innovation. As the genre evolved, the Fado Houses became the laboratories where new styles, techniques, and vocal interpretations were explored and experimented with. This delicate balance between honoring tradition and embracing change allowed Fado to adapt and thrive, ensuring its relevance and appeal across generations.

As Fado gained prominence within Portuguese society, a pantheon of iconic performers began to emerge, each leaving an indelible mark on the evolution of the genre. These individuals, through their distinctive vocal styles, instrumental mastery, and emotional interpretations, became the torchbearers of the Fado tradition, captivating audiences both domestically and internationally.

One of the most revered Fado icons was the legendary Maria Severa, a figure whose life and artistry have become the stuff of legend. Born in the mid-19th century, Severa's powerful and emotive voice, coupled with her captivating stage presence, elevated Fado to new heights of artistry and popularity. Her influence on subsequent generations of Fado performers is a testament to the enduring impact she had on the genre.

Another iconic Fado figure was Amália Rodrigues, often referred to as the "Queen of Fado." Rodrigues' rich, velvety voice and her ability to imbue each performance with a profound sense of melancholy and introspection cemented her status as one of the most celebrated and influential Fado artists of all time. Her recordings and live performances have become the benchmark by which contemporary Fado artists are measured, and her legacy continues to inspire and shape the evolution of the genre.

The rise of these legendary Fado performers not only solidified the genre's place within the cultural fabric of Portugal but also paved the way for future generations of artists to push the boundaries of the art form. Through their artistry and dedication, the iconic Fado performers ensured that the genre would endure and continue to captivate audiences for decades to come.

As Fado gained widespread recognition and acclaim, the genre began to transcend its humble origins in the Fado Houses and the cobblestone streets of Lisbon. The democratization of Fado, a process that unfolded over the 20th century, saw the genre transition from a marginalized art form to one that commanded the attention of the cultural elite and the masses alike.

This transformation was driven by a confluence of factors, including the increasing popularity of Fado recordings, the emergence of acclaimed Fado performers on the national and international stage, and the growing appreciation for the genre's artistic merits within the broader societal context.

The advent of radio and the recording industry played a pivotal role in the democratization of Fado. As the genre's iconic performers began to release recordings that were widely accessible to the public, the allure of Fado spread beyond the confines of the Fado Houses, reaching new audiences and cementing its status as a cultural touchstone.

Furthermore, the establishment of prestigious Fado performance venues, such as the legendary Casa da Severa in Lisbon, further elevated the genre's stature. These venues, which combined the intimate ambiance of the traditional Fado Houses with the grandeur of concert halls, attracted a diverse audience, from working-class citizens to the intellectual and artistic elite.

The democratization of Fado also led to the genre's cross-pollination with other musical styles, further expanding its reach and appeal. Fado artists began to experiment with elements of jazz, pop, and world music, creating captivating hybrid forms that resonated with a broader demographic.

This process of democratization, while not without its challenges and controversies, ultimately served to cement Fado's position as a vital and enduring component of Portugal's cultural identity. The genre's transition from the margins to the mainstream not only broadened its audience but also ensured its continued relevance and evolution in the face of a rapidly changing cultural landscape.

As the 20th century drew to a close, Fado's influence and appeal extended far beyond the borders of Portugal, captivating audiences around the world and solidifying its status as a global phenomenon.

The rise of acclaimed Fado performers, such as Amália Rodrigues and Mariza, played a pivotal role in this international expansion.

These artists, through their mesmerizing live performances and critically acclaimed recordings, introduced the captivating sound of Fado to new audiences, sparking a growing interest and appreciation for the genre.

The global resonance of Fado was further amplified by its incorporation into various artistic mediums, including film, television, and theater. The haunting melodies and evocative lyrics of Fado found their way into the soundtracks of acclaimed international productions, exposing the genre to new demographics and fostering a deeper understanding of its emotional and cultural significance.

Moreover, the establishment of Fado festivals and cultural events around the world, from the United States to Japan, served as a testament to the genre's universal appeal. These gatherings not only celebrated the artistry of Fado but also provided a platform for cultural exchange, allowing the genre to transcend geographical boundaries and connect people from diverse backgrounds.

The global recognition of Fado as an intangible cultural heritage of humanity by UNESCO in 2011 further solidified its status as a cherished and irreplaceable component of the world's cultural tapestry. This prestigious designation not only highlighted the genre's artistic and historical significance but also underscored the enduring power of Fado to captivate and inspire audiences across the globe.

As Fado continues to evolve and adapt to the ever-changing cultural landscape, its global reach and influence only seem to expand. The genre's ability to resonate with audiences, regardless of their cultural or national origins, is a testament to the universal human experiences it encapsulates – a shared sense of melancholy, resilience, and the profound connection to one's roots.

The story of Fado is not merely a tale of a musical genre; it is a testament to the resilience, depth, and enduring spirit of the Portuguese people. This captivating art form, born from the cobblestone streets of Lisbon and nurtured within the intimate confines of the Fado Houses, has transcended the boundaries of time and space to become a cherished cultural icon that defines the very essence of Portugal.

As the origins and evolution of Fado unfold, we bear witness to the profound interplay between tradition and innovation, where the preservation of a rich musical legacy coexists with the constant reimagining and reinterpretation of the genre. This delicate balance, this eternal dance between the old and the new, is what has allowed Fado to remain relevant and captivating, even in the face of a rapidly changing world.

At its core, Fado is a reflection of the human experience – a tapestry woven with threads of melancholy, resilience, and a profound connection to one's roots. It is a musical genre that speaks to the universal language of the soul, transcending cultural and linguistic boundaries to touch the hearts of audiences across the globe.

As we delve deeper into the origins and evolution of Fado, we are confronted with the realization that this art form is not merely a product of Portugal's musical heritage; it is a testament to the indomitable spirit of the Portuguese people – a spirit that has weathered the storms of history, emerged stronger, and continues to captivate the world with its soulful and evocative melodies.

The story of Fado is a testament to the power of art to preserve, reflect, and shape the cultural identity of a nation. It is a reminder that the most profound and enduring forms of expression are often those that emerge from the collective experiences and shared emotions of a people, distilled into the timeless medium of music.

As we continue to explore and appreciate the origins and evolution of Fado, we must also recognize the vital role it plays in the cultural fabric of Portugal. For Fado is not merely a genre of music; it is the very soul of a nation, a tapestry of stories, emotions, and the indomitable human spirit that continues to resonate with audiences around the world.

At the very heart of Fado lies its iconic melodic structure, a captivating tapestry of wistful, melancholic tones that have become the sonic signature of the genre. The Fado melody, often described as a lament, is characterized by its undulating contours, which rise and fall with a sense of poignant yearning, evoking a profound emotional response from the listener.

The distinctive Fado melody is rooted in the historical and cultural influences that have shaped the genre over the centuries. Drawing inspiration from the melancholic ballads of the Iberian Peninsula, as well as the soulful laments of the African diaspora, the Fado melody has evolved into a singular form that is instantly recognizable and deeply resonant.

One of the hallmarks of the Fado melody is its emphasis on the minor key, which lends the music a sense of introspective melancholy. This harmonic structure, combined with the plaintive, emotive delivery of the vocals, creates a sonic landscape that is simultaneously introspective and universally relatable. The listener is invited to empathize with the emotional narratives woven into the music, to feel the weight of sorrow and the glimmer of hope that coexist within the Fado experience.

Moreover, the Fado melody is often characterized by its use of melismatic phrasing, where a single syllable is stretched across multiple notes. This technique, which is deeply rooted in the musical traditions of the Iberian Peninsula, serves to heighten the emotional intensity of the lyrics, infusing each word with a sense of profound significance and personal resonance.

The captivating interplay between the minor-key melodies, the melismatic vocal delivery, and the evocative lyrical content is what sets Fado apart as a truly unique and powerful musical form. The haunting, mesmerizing quality of the Fado melody can transport the listener to a realm of profound emotional experience, where the boundaries between the individual and the collective dissolve, and the shared human experience is laid bare for all to witness.

Interwoven with the captivating melodies of Fado are the poetic narratives that serve as the foundation for the genre's thematic depth and emotional resonance. The lyrics of Fado, often referred to as "Poesia Cantada" (Sung Poetry), are the vessels through which the Portuguese people express their deepest desires, fears, and experiences.

The themes that permeate the lyrics of Fado are as diverse as the human condition itself, spanning the spectrum of love, loss, longing, and the enduring struggle against the vicissitudes of life. From the bittersweet tales of unrequited love to the poignant lamentations of those who have weathered the storms of adversity, the Fado lyrical canon is a tapestry of universal human experiences that transcend the boundaries of time and place.

One of the most prominent themes that emerge from the Fado lyrics is the concept of "saudade," a quintessentially Portuguese word that defies direct translation but is often described as a profound sense of melancholic longing, a deep-seated yearning for that which is absent or lost. This thematic undercurrent is woven throughout the Fado repertoire, imbuing the music with a palpable sense of emotional depth and personal resonance.

The Fado lyricists, often revered as the unsung poets of the Portuguese nation, possess a remarkable ability to distill the complexities of the human experience into evocative, poetic language. Through their masterful use of metaphor, symbolism, and vivid imagery, these lyrical artisans craft narratives that resonate on a profoundly personal level, allowing the listener to connect with the universal themes that underpin the Fado tradition.

Moreover, the Fado lyrics often serve as a

conduit for the expression of social commentary and political critique, providing a platform for the voicing of the collective experiences and struggles of the Portuguese people. From the lamentations of the working class to the defiant proclamations of the marginalized, the Fado lyrical canon has long been a vehicle for the articulation of the unheard voices within Portuguese society.

The Fado lyrical narratives, in their multifaceted complexity, serve as a testament to the enduring power of the human spirit, a testament to the resilience and perseverance that have long been the hallmarks of the Portuguese nation. Through the evocative words and profound emotional resonance of the Fado lyrics, the listener is invited to embark on a journey of self-reflection, to confront the universal truths that bind us all as human beings.

At the heart of the Fado tradition lies the captivating and deeply intimate performance experience, a ritual that has been honed and refined over the centuries to create a sense of profound emotional connection between the artist and the audience.

The Fado performance, often taking place in the dimly lit and cozy confines of the traditional

Fado Houses, is a meticulously curated endeavor that invites the audience to become active participants in the unfolding of the musical narrative. The performer, be it a vocalist or an instrumentalist, is not merely a passive conduit for the music; rather, they are the conduits through which the emotional essence of Fado is channeled and expressed.

The Fado performer, through their mastery of vocal technique and emotional interpretation, becomes the embodiment of the genre's thematic tapestry, weaving together the haunting melodies and the poetic narratives to create a transcendent experience for the audience. The artist's ability to convey the depth of emotion inherent in the Fado tradition, to channel the collective sorrow and resilience of the Portuguese people, is what sets the Fado performance apart as a truly mesmerizing and transformative experience.

The intimate nature of the Fado performance is further accentuated by the unique performance dynamic that unfolds between the artist and the audience. Rather than a detached, one-way exchange, the Fado performance is characterized by a palpable sense of mutual exchange and emotional investment. The audience, through their rapt attention, their audible gasps of empathy, and their enthusiastic response, become active participants in the unfolding of the musical narrative, creating a symbiotic and deeply immersive experience.

Moreover, the Fado performance is often enhanced by the presence of traditional Fado instrumentation, such as the Portuguese guitar and the classical guitar, which serve to provide a rich, textural accompaniment to the evocative vocals. The interplay between the melodic lines of the instruments and the emotive delivery of the vocals creates a sonic tapestry that is at once captivating and deeply personal, inviting the listener to become fully immersed in the emotional landscape of the Fado experience.

The Fado performance, with its emphasis on intimacy, emotional intensity, and the symbiotic relationship between the artist and the audience, is a testament to the enduring power of live music to transcend the boundaries of the every day and transport the listener to a realm of profound emotional resonance. It is a ritual that has been carefully curated and preserved over the centuries, serving as a vital link between the past and the present, and ensuring the continued vitality and relevance of the Fado tradition.

Fado, as a multifaceted artistic form, is not merely a musical genre; it is a captivating tapestry of visual and aesthetic elements that

---

serve to enhance and amplify the emotional resonance of the music. From the dimly lit ambiance of the Fado Houses to the sartorial choices of the performers, the Fado aesthetic is a carefully cultivated expression of the genre's thematic underpinnings, inviting the audience to fully immerse themselves in the emotional landscape of the Portuguese musical tradition.

At the core of the Fado aesthetic is the embrace of melancholy, a profound acknowledgment of the bittersweet realities of the human experience. The dimly lit performance spaces, the muted color palettes, and the somber, introspective demeanor of the performers all contribute to the creation of a mood that is at once somber and deeply evocative. This melancholic aesthetic serves to heighten the emotional intensity of the Fado experience, inviting the audience to engage with the music on a profoundly personal level.

Yet, the Fado aesthetic is not solely defined by its melancholic undertones; it also encompasses a sense of the sublime, a reverence for the grandeur and the majesty of the human spirit. The elegant, formal attire of the Fado performers, often adorned with intricate embroidery and ornamental details, serves to imbue the genre with a sense of dignity and timeless elegance. This aesthetic juxtaposition, between the melancholic and the sublime, creates a visual tapestry that mirrors the emotional depth and complexity inherent in the Fado tradition.

Moreover, the Fado aesthetic extends beyond the confines of the performance spaces, manifesting in the broader cultural landscape of Portugal. The iconic black-and-white garments worn by Fado performers, particularly the traditional mantilla and the black shawl, have become sartorial symbols of the genre, serving as a visual representation of the genre's enduring significance within the national consciousness.

The Fado aesthetic, in its multifaceted complexity, serves as a powerful statement of the genre's cultural significance and its ability to transcend the boundaries of the purely musical. By seamlessly blending the melancholic and the sublime, the Fado aesthetic invites the audience to engage with the genre on a holistic level, connecting the auditory experience with the visual and the emotional.

Through the careful cultivation of this aesthetic, the Fado tradition has established itself as a unique and captivating artistic form that resonates not only with the Portuguese people but with audiences around the world. The Fado aesthetic, in its evocative and emotionally charged manifestation, serves as a testament to the enduring power of art to shape and reflect the cultural identity of a nation.

As we delve into the multifaceted characteristics and thematic underpinnings of Fado, we are confronted with the realization that this captivating musical genre is not merely a product of Portugal's cultural heritage; it is a living, breathing entity that continues to evolve and adapt to the changing tides of the modern world.

The enduring legacy of Fado is rooted in its ability to serve as a conduit for the expression of the human experience, a musical form that transcends the boundaries of time and place to resonate with audiences across the globe. Whether it is the haunting melodies that evoke a profound sense of melancholy, the poetic narratives that give voice to the collective experiences of the Portuguese people, or the intimate and immersive performance dynamics that invite the audience to become active participants in the unfolding of the musical story, Fado remains a captivating and enduring art form that continues to captivate and inspire.

As the Fado tradition continues to evolve, embracing new interpretations and innovative approaches, it serves as a testament to the resilience and adaptability of the Portuguese spirit. The genre's ability to remain relevant and resonant in the face of a rapidly changing cultural landscape is a testament to the enduring power of art to shape and reflect the collective identity of a nation.

Moreover, the global recognition and acclaim that Fado has garnered in recent decades, culminating in its designation as an Intangible Cultural Heritage of Humanity by UNESCO in 2011, serves as a powerful affirmation of the genre's universal appeal and its ability to transcend the boundaries of national and cultural identity. The Fado tradition, with its deep roots in the Iberian Peninsula, has become a cherished component of the global cultural tapestry, a testament to the enduring power of music to forge connections and foster a deeper understanding of the human experience.

As we continue to explore and engage with the captivating world of Fado, we are reminded of the profound and enduring impact that this musical genre has had on the cultural landscape of Portugal and the world at large. The characteristics and themes that define Fado – the haunting melodies, the poetic narratives, the intimate performance dynamics, and the evocative aesthetic – serve as a testament to the power of art to capture the essence of the human experience, to give voice to the collective aspirations and struggles of a people, and to transcend the boundaries of time and space.

The enduring legacy of Fado is not merely a testament to the enduring power of the Portuguese musical tradition; it is a reflection of the indomitable human spirit, a testament to the timeless and universal truths that bind us all as members of the global community. As we continue to explore and engage with this captivating art form, we are invited to embark on a journey of self-discovery, confront the complexities of the human experience, and find solace and inspiration in the timeless and evocative melodies of Fado.

PORTUGUESE GUITAR

In the captivating world of Portuguese music, one instrument stands out as the quintessential embodiment of the nation's cultural identity: the Portuguese guitar, a truly remarkable and uniquely crafted instrument that has become inextricably linked with the enduring legacy of Fado, the soulful musical genre that has long been regarded as the very heart and soul of Portugal.

To delve into the history and construction of the Portuguese guitar is to embark on a journey of profound cultural significance, a tale that weaves together the threads of Portugal's rich musical heritage, the ingenious craftsmanship of its luthiers, and the timeless artistry of the musicians who have mastered its ethereal, yet distinctive, sound. This instrument, with its captivating contours and meticulously engineered design, has not only shaped the musical landscape of Portugal but has also captivated audiences around the world, serving as a tangible representation of the nation's cultural identity and the enduring power of music to transcend geographical boundaries.

The origins of the Portuguese guitar can be traced back to the rich tapestry of musical influences that have converged within the Iberian Peninsula over centuries. While the precise origins of this distinctive instrument remain shrouded in a veil of historical uncertainty, scholars and musicians have pieced together a narrative that offers valuable insights into the formative stages of the Portuguese guitar's evolution.

One of the most widely accepted theories suggests that the Portuguese guitar can be traced back to the arrival of the Arabic lute, the oud, on the Iberian Peninsula during the

Moorish occupation of the region. This instrument, with its distinctive teardrop-shaped body and intricate sound, is believed to have served as a foundational inspiration for the development of the Portuguese guitar, as the local craftsmen and musicians sought to adapt and reinterpret the foreign instrument to better suit the musical traditions of the region.

As the Iberian Peninsula underwent a cultural and religious transformation, with the gradual expulsion of the Moors and the rise of the Christian kingdoms, the instrument that would eventually become the Portuguese guitar began to take shape. Influenced by the Spanish vihuela, a Renaissance-era plucked string instrument, as well as the traditional folk instruments of the region, the Portuguese guitar emerged as a unique and distinctive musical entity, characterized by its distinctive pear-shaped body, intricate sound, and captivating melodies it would come to produce.

The pivotal moment in the Portuguese guitar's history came during the 18th century when the instrument underwent a significant transformation that would cement its status as a truly unique and defining element of Portuguese musical culture. It was during this period that the instrument's construction was refined and standardized, with the introduction of the distinctive twelve-string configuration that became the hallmark of the Portuguese guitar.

This crucial innovation, attributed to the skilled luthiers and master craftsmen of the era, not only enhanced the instrument's tonal range and expressive capabilities but also imbued it with a sonic signature that would become inextricably linked with the burgeoning Fado tradition. As the Portuguese guitar became an integral component of Fado performances, its distinctive sound and captivating melodies would come to captivate audiences both within the nation's borders and beyond.

The Portuguese guitar, with its distinctive pear-shaped body and intricate twelve-string configuration, is a meticulously engineered musical instrument that is the product of centuries of refinement and innovation. To fully understand the significance and the uniqueness of this instrument, it is essential to delve into the intricacies of its construction, exploring the various components and the craftsmanship that have shaped its iconic design.

At the heart of the Portuguese guitar lies its distinctive body, a pear-shaped resonating chamber that is crafted with the utmost care and attention to detail. The body of the instrument is typically constructed from a combination of carefully selected woods, with the soundboard, or the top of the instrument, often made from spruce or cedar, and the back and sides fashioned from a variety of hardwoods, such as rosewood or maple.

The curvaceous contours of the Portuguese guitar's body are not merely an aesthetic choice; they serve a crucial functional purpose, enhancing the instrument's tonal qualities and projecting the captivating melodies that have become the hallmark of the Fado tradition. The precise shaping and dimensioning of the body, meticulously calculated by the skilled luthiers, are essential in creating the instrument's distinctive sound, which is characterized by its rich, resonant tone and the subtle nuances that allow it to seamlessly integrate with the emotive vocals and intricate guitar accompaniment of Fado.

Atop the Portuguese guitar's body sits the instrument's neck, a slender and elegantly tapered component that serves as the foundation for the instrument's twelve strings. The neck, typically constructed from hardwoods such as mahogany or maple, is carefully designed to provide the player with optimal comfort and control, allowing them to navigate the intricate chord progressions and melismatic flourishes that are so integral to the Fado performance.

The most distinctive and defining feature of the Portuguese guitar, however, is its unique twelve-string configuration. This arrangement, which sets the instrument apart from its six-string counterparts, is the result of centuries of experimentation and refinement by the nation's luthiers. The twelve strings, which are typically arranged in six double-string courses, create a rich, complex, and ethereal sound that is instantly recognizable as the signature of the Portuguese guitar.

The meticulous craftsmanship and attention to detail that go into the construction of the Portuguese guitar are not merely aesthetic concerns; they are essential in shaping the instrument's unique sonic qualities. From the precise curvature of the body to the carefully engineered neck and the intricate string arrangement, every aspect of the Portuguese guitar's design is meticulously considered and executed to ensure the instrument's ability to captivate and inspire audiences through the timeless melodies of the Fado tradition.

The Portuguese guitar, with its captivating sound and distinctive appearance, has become inextricably linked with the enduring legacy of Fado, the soulful musical genre that is widely regarded as the quintessential embodiment of Portugal's cultural identity. As the Fado tradition has evolved and adapted over the centuries, the Portuguese guitar has remained a constant and integral component, serving as a vital conduit for the expression of the genre's emotive narratives and the preservation of its musical heritage.

At the heart of the Fado performance, the Portuguese guitar assumes a pivotal role, serving as the rhythmic and harmonic foundation upon which the captivating melodies and poetic lyrics are built. The skilled Fado guitarists, through their mastery of the instrument's intricate techniques and their ability to seamlessly blend the twelve-string configuration with the emotive vocals, become the conduits through which the essence of Fado is channeled and expressed.

The Portuguese guitar's contribution to the Fado tradition extends far beyond its role as a mere accompaniment; it is an essential element that shapes the very character and emotional resonance of the music. The instrument's rich, resonant tone and its ability to imbue each performance with a sense of melancholic longing and resilience are what lend Fado its distinctive sonic signature and its profound emotional impact.

Moreover, the Portuguese guitar's intimate

connection to the Fado tradition is not merely a functional one; it is a symbiotic relationship that has been cultivated and nurtured throughout generations. The sight of a Fado performer, guitar in hand, has become a powerful visual representation of the genre's enduring legacy, a tangible embodiment of the deep-rooted cultural heritage that defines the Portuguese nation.

As the Fado tradition has evolved and adapted to the changing tides of the modern world, the role of the Portuguese guitar has also transformed. Contemporary Fado artists have increasingly experimented with the instrument, exploring new techniques and incorporating it into innovative musical arrangements that blend the genre's traditional elements with contemporary influences. This dynamic interplay between tradition and innovation has served to further cement the Portuguese guitar's status as a vital and enduring component of the Fado tradition, ensuring its continued relevance and appeal in the 21st century and beyond.

As the Portuguese guitar has become an integral part of the nation's cultural heritage, the preservation and perpetuation of its tradition have become a matter of paramount importance. The intricate craftsmanship and the deep-rooted significance of this instrument have inspired a dedicated community of luthiers, musicians, and enthusiasts to ensure that the art of Portuguese guitar-making and performance remains a vital and thriving component of Portugal's cultural identity.

At the forefront of this effort are the skilled luthiers, the master craftsmen who have dedicated their lives to the preservation and evolution of the Portuguese guitar. These individuals, drawing upon centuries-old techniques and the accumulated wisdom of their predecessors, have meticulously honed their craft, ensuring that the instrument's distinctive design and sound are faithfully maintained and passed down to future generations.

The luthiers' commitment to the preservation of the Portuguese guitar tradition extends beyond the mere construction of the instrument; it involves a deep understanding of the instrument's history, the nuances of its construction, and the techniques required to coax its captivating melodies from the carefully selected and crafted components. Through their tireless work, these artisans have become the custodians of a cultural legacy that transcends the boundaries of mere musical instrument-making, becoming the guardians of a cherished national treasure.

Alongside the luthiers, the Fado musicians themselves have played a crucial role in the perpetuation of the Portuguese guitar tradition. These skilled performers, who have dedicated their lives to the mastery of the instrument and its integration into the Fado tradition, have become the torchbearers of a legacy that stretches back generations. Through their dynamic performances, their innovative interpretations, and their commitment to passing on their knowledge and expertise to the next generation of musicians, the Fado artists have ensured that the Portuguese guitar remains a vital and integral component of the nation's cultural landscape.

The preservation and perpetuation of the Portuguese guitar tradition have also been bolstered by the establishment of educational institutions and cultural organizations dedicated to the instrument's study and appreciation. From specialized guitar-making schools to Fado academies and cultural centers, these initiatives have provided aspiring musicians and luthiers with the resources and support necessary to hone their craft, ensuring that the art of the Portuguese guitar continues to thrive and evolve.

As the Portuguese guitar continues to captivate and inspire audiences around the world, the efforts of the dedicated community of luthiers, musicians, and cultural advocates have become increasingly vital. By safeguarding the instrument's heritage, fostering its growth, and ensuring its continued relevance in the face of a rapidly changing cultural landscape, these individuals have become the guardians of a national treasure, ensuring that the distinctive sound of the Portuguese guitar will continue to resonate for generations to come.

The humble yet captivating Portuguese guitar, with its distinctive design and soul-stirring sound, has transcended the borders of the Iberian Peninsula to become a global phenomenon, captivating audiences and inspiring musicians across the world. As the instrument's fame and influence have grown, it has become a powerful ambassador for the rich cultural heritage of Portugal, serving as a tangible representation of the nation's enduring musical legacy.

The global impact of the Portuguese guitar can be traced back to the international recognition and acclaim garnered by the Fado tradition, of which the instrument has become an integral component. As Fado gained recognition as a UNESCO Intangible Cultural Heritage of Humanity, the Portuguese guitar's significance as a vital component of this cherished art form was also thrust into the global spotlight.

Beyond the realm of Fado, the Portuguese guitar has found its way into the musical repertoires of diverse genres and styles, captivating audiences and inspiring collaborations that have served to further expand the instrument's reach and influence. From the fusion of traditional Portuguese music with contemporary sounds to the incorporation of the Portuguese guitar into the compositions of international artists, the instrument has proven its ability to transcend cultural boundaries and resonate with audiences across the globe.

The growing international fascination with the Portuguese guitar has also led to the establishment of educational programs and cultural initiatives that aim to foster a deeper understanding and appreciation of the instrument's history, construction, and role within the broader context of Portuguese musical heritage. From specialized workshops and masterclasses to the creation of dedicated performance venues and festivals, these efforts have played a pivotal role in introducing the Portuguese guitar to new audiences and ensuring its continued relevance on the global stage.

Furthermore, the increasing availability of high-quality recordings and digital media featuring the Portuguese guitar has also contributed to its widespread popularity and recognition. The ability of listeners around the world to access the captivating sound of the instrument, whether through the recordings of renowned Fado artists or the innovative interpretations of international musicians, has served to amplify the Portuguese guitar's global impact and solidify its status as a cherished cultural icon.

As the Portuguese guitar continues to captivate and inspire audiences across the globe, its significance extends far beyond the realm of music. The instrument has become a powerful symbol of Portugal's rich cultural heritage, a tangible representation of the nation's resilience, creativity, and enduring spirit.

Through the global dissemination and appreciation of the Portuguese guitar, the world is granted a window into the very soul of Portugal, a profound cultural exchange that has the power to transcend linguistic and geographical barriers.

The enduring legacy of the Portuguese guitar, with its ability to captivate and inspire audiences worldwide, is a testament to the transformative power of music and the enduring significance of cultural traditions. As the instrument continues to evolve and adapt, embracing new interpretations and collaborations, it serves as a shining example of how cultural heritage can be preserved, celebrated, and shared with the world, forging connections and fostering a deeper understanding of the human experience.

In the captivating realm of Portuguese music, the role of the virtuoso guitarist has long been pivotal, serving as the conduit through which the soulful essence of the nation's cherished musical traditions is channeled and expressed. These remarkable individuals, wielding the distinctive Portuguese guitar with unparalleled mastery, have not only captivated audiences both within and beyond the borders of the Iberian Peninsula but have also become the living embodiments of a cultural legacy that stretches back through the centuries.

As we delve into the lives and techniques of the most renowned Portuguese guitarists, we find ourselves confronted with a tapestry of artistry, innovation, and an unwavering commitment to the preservation and evolution of a hallowed musical tradition. From the iconic figures who have indelibly etched their names into the annals of Fado history to the contemporary virtuosos who have pushed the boundaries of the instrument's capabilities, each of these remarkable musicians has played a vital role in shaping the sonic landscape of Portugal's musical heritage.

At the forefront of the Portuguese guitar's

enduring legacy stand the pioneering figures who have dedicated their lives to the mastery and advancement of this remarkable instrument. These individuals, through their virtuosic performances, innovative techniques, and unwavering commitment to the preservation of their nation's musical heritage, have become the revered custodians of a tradition that has captivated audiences across the globe.

One such pioneer is the esteemed Artur Paredes, a legendary figure whose name has become synonymous with the very essence of the Portuguese guitar. Paredes, born in the late 19th century, is widely regarded as the individual who standardized and codified the instrument's distinctive twelve-string configuration, establishing the blueprint that would shape the sound and construction of the Portuguese guitar for generations to come.

Through his meticulous attention to detail, his innovative approach to technique, and his tireless efforts to disseminate the art of Portuguese guitar-playing, Paredes became a towering figure within the nation's musical landscape. His virtuosic performances, which seamlessly blended the traditional elements of the instrument with his creative interpretations, captivated audiences and inspired a legion of devoted followers who sought to emulate his mastery.

Alongside Paredes, another pioneering figure who has left an indelible mark on the Portuguese guitar tradition is the revered Carlos Paredes, a musician whose name has become synonymous with the very soul of Fado. As the son of the legendary Artur Paredes, Carlos inherited not only the technical prowess of his father but also the deep-rooted connection to the emotional resonance of the Portuguese guitar, imbuing his performances with a profound sense of personal and cultural significance.

Through his dynamic and emotive interpretations of Fado classics, Carlos Paredes became a towering figure within the genre, his nimble fingers coaxing from the Portuguese guitar a sonic tapestry that was at once hauntingly melancholic and triumphantly resilient. His influence on subsequent generations of guitarists cannot be overstated, as his artistry and innovation became the benchmarks against which all others were measured.

These pioneering figures, Artur Paredes and Carlos Paredes, represent the cornerstones upon which the enduring legacy of the Portuguese guitar has been built. Their unwavering dedication to the instrument, their mastery of its technical nuances, and their ability to imbue their performances with a profound sense of emotional resonance have cemented their status as the revered custodians of a musical tradition that continues to captivate and inspire audiences across the globe.

As the Portuguese guitar tradition has continued to evolve and adapt to the changing tides of the modern musical landscape, a new generation of virtuosos has emerged, poised to carry the torch of this hallowed instrument into the future. These remarkable musicians, drawing upon the rich legacy of their predecessors while embracing innovative techniques and interpretive approaches, have become the torchbearers of a tradition that continues to captivate and inspire audiences both within and beyond the borders of Portugal.

One such contemporary virtuoso is the acclaimed Gaspar Varela, a musician whose technical prowess and artistic vision have earned him international acclaim. Varela, through his dynamic and captivating performances, has become renowned for his ability to seamlessly blend the traditional elements of the Portuguese guitar with contemporary influences, creating a sonic tapestry that is both deeply rooted in the nation's musical heritage and strikingly innovative.

Varela's mastery of the instrument is evident in his command of the Portuguese guitar's distinctive twelve-string configuration, his nimble fingers coaxing from the instrument a rich, resonant sound that serves as the foundation for his emotive and technically demanding interpretations. Moreover, his ability to imbue his performances with a profound sense of personal expression and cultural significance has cemented his status as a leading figure within the contemporary Portuguese guitar landscape.

Another contemporary virtuoso who has made an indelible mark on the Portuguese guitar tradition is the remarkable Custódio Castelo. Castelo, a musician whose technical prowess and interpretive artistry have earned him global recognition, has become renowned for his ability to push the boundaries of the instrument, exploring new techniques and innovative approaches that have served to expand the sonic and expressive capabilities of the Portuguese guitar.

Through his dynamic and captivating performances, Castelo has not only captivated audiences with his virtuosic command of the instrument but has also become a tireless advocate for the preservation and continued evolution of the Portuguese guitar tradition. His dedication to passing on his knowledge and expertise to the next generation of guitarists has ensured that the rich legacy of this hallowed instrument will continue to thrive and evolve in the years to come.

These contemporary virtuosos, Gaspar Varela and Custódio Castelo, are just two examples of the remarkable musicians who have emerged to carry the torch of the Portuguese guitar tradition into the 21st century. Their unwavering commitment to the mastery of their craft, their innovative approaches to technique and interpretation, and their deep-rooted connection to the cultural significance of the instrument have cemented their status as the leading figures in the ongoing evolution of this captivating musical form.

Through their dynamic and emotive performances, these contemporary virtuosos have not only captivated audiences around the world but have also served as ambassadors for the rich cultural heritage of Portugal, showcasing the enduring power and relevance of the Portuguese guitar in the modern era.

At the heart of the Portuguese guitar's enduring legacy lies the intricate and meticulously honed techniques that have been developed and refined by generations of virtuoso performers. These distinctive approaches to the instrument, which have been passed down through the centuries, have become the cornerstone of the Portuguese guitar's unique sonic signature and its ability to captivate and emote.

One of the most renowned and distinctive techniques associated with the Portuguese guitar is the "rasgueado," a percussive strumming pattern that is characterized by the rapid, rhythmic brushing of the strings. This technique, which is deeply rooted in the Iberian musical traditions, serves to imbue the instrument's sound with a pulsating, percussive energy that complements the emotive vocals and intricate harmonies of the Fado genre.

The mastery of the "rasgueado" technique requires a level of dexterity and coordination that is truly remarkable, as the guitarist must precisely control the movement of their fingers to produce the desired rhythmic patterns and tonal qualities. Through the meticulous practice and honing of this technique, Portuguese guitarists have not only become renowned for their technical prowess but have also developed a deep understanding of the instrument's expressive potential, using the "rasgueado" as a means of conveying the emotional essence of the music.

Another distinctive technique that has become synonymous with the Portuguese guitar is the "tirando," a delicate and intricate fingerpicking pattern that allows the musician to coax a rich, resonant sound from the instrument's twelve strings. This technique, which requires a high degree of precision and control, serves to highlight the instrument's harmonies and melodic contours, creating a sonic tapestry that is both captivating and deeply emotive.

The mastery of the "tirando" technique is not merely a technical feat; it is a reflection of the guitarist's deep understanding of the Portuguese guitar's tonal qualities and their ability to harness these nuances to enhance the emotional resonance of their performances. Through the deft manipulation of the instrument's strings, Portuguese guitarists can imbue their music with a sense of intimacy and personal expression that is truly captivating.

Beyond these established techniques, contemporary Portuguese guitarists have also begun to explore innovative approaches to the instrument, pushing the boundaries of what is considered traditional and introducing new ways of harnessing the expressive potential of the Portuguese guitar. From the incorporation of extended techniques, such as the use of harmonics and percussive slapping, to the exploration of unconventional chord voicings and harmonic structures, these musicians have demonstrated a remarkable capacity for innovation and a deep commitment to the continued evolution of their nation's musical heritage.

The techniques and approaches employed by the notable Portuguese guitarists, whether rooted in tradition or embracing the spirit of innovation, serve as a testament to the remarkable artistry and dedication that has been poured into the mastery of this hallowed instrument. Through the meticulous honing of their craft and the constant exploration of new expressive possibilities, these musicians have become the custodians of a cultural legacy that continues to captivate and inspire audiences around the world.

As the remarkable Portuguese guitarists have continued to push the boundaries of their craft, their impact and global recognition have grown exponentially, solidifying the instrument's status as a cherished component of the world's cultural heritage. From the iconic figures who have become synonymous with the very essence of Fado to the contemporary virtuosos who have introduced the Portuguese guitar to new and diverse audiences, these remarkable musicians have played a pivotal role in the dissemination and appreciation of this captivating musical tradition.

One of the most significant markers of the Portuguese guitar virtuosos' global impact has been their recognition on the international stage. The prestigious accolades and awards bestowed upon these remarkable musicians, from prestigious global music competitions to the prestigious UNESCO designation of Fado as an Intangible Cultural Heritage of Humanity, have served to shine a spotlight on the enduring significance of the Portuguese guitar and the artistry of those who have dedicated their lives to its mastery.

Moreover, the growing international collaborations and cross-cultural exchanges that have involved the Portuguese guitar virtuosos have further amplified the instrument's global reach and impact. These musicians have not only captivated audiences within the confines of the Iberian Peninsula but have also forged connections with artists and musical traditions from around the world, creating dynamic and innovative fusions that have served to introduce the captivating sound of the Portuguese guitar to new and diverse demographics.

The global recognition and impact of the Portuguese guitar virtuosos have also manifested in the increasing demand for their performances and recordings on the international stage. From sold-out concerts in major concert halls to the widespread availability of their music on global streaming platforms, these remarkable musicians have become the de facto ambassadors for the rich cultural heritage of Portugal, sharing the enduring legacy of the Portuguese guitar with audiences across the globe.

Furthermore, the influence of the Portuguese guitar virtuosos can be seen in the growing number of aspiring musicians and luthiers who have been inspired to take up the instrument and dedicate themselves to the preservation and evolution of this hallowed tradition. The mentorship and educational initiatives spearheaded by these remarkable individuals have played a crucial role in ensuring that the art of Portuguese guitar-playing continues to thrive and evolve, passing the torch to the next generation of custodians.

As the global impact and recognition of the Portuguese guitar virtuosos continue to grow, their significance extends far beyond the realm of music. These remarkable individuals have become the ambassadors of a cultural legacy that transcends the boundaries of the Iberian Peninsula, serving as the conduits through which the rich tapestry of Portugal's musical heritage is shared with the world. Through their artistry, dedication, and unwavering commitment to the preservation and evolution of the Portuguese guitar, these virtuosos have cemented the instrument's status as a cherished component of the global cultural landscape.

151

BOSSA NOVA

In the intricate and diverse landscape of world music, few genres have emerged as prominently as Bossa Nova, captivating audiences with its unique blend of rhythm, melody, and cultural heritage. This mesmerizing genre has etched its place in the collective consciousness, evoking a sense of romance, sophistication, and authenticity that few other genres can rival. Originating from the sun-kissed shores of Brazil, this enchanting fusion of jazz, samba, and the melancholic sensibilities of the Portuguese-speaking world has transcended its geographic origins to become a universal language of emotion and artistic expression.

Yet, the story of Bossa Nova's impact on the musical landscape of Portugal is one of captivating complexity, a tale that weaves together the threads of cultural exchange, artistic innovation, and the enduring bonds that tie the Lusophone nations together. As the rhythmic pulse and lyrical nuances of Bossa Nova permeated the musical consciousness of Portugal, the nation's rich musical heritage underwent a remarkable metamorphosis, giving birth to a vibrant and ever-evolving tapestry of sound that continues to captivate audiences and inspire musicians the world over.

To fully comprehend the profound impact of Bossa Nova on the musical traditions of Portugal, we must first explore the origins and foundations of this captivating genre within its Brazilian homeland. Emerging in the late 1950s, Bossa Nova was born from the confluence of several distinct musical traditions, each of which contributed to the genre's unique sonic signature and its ability to captivate audiences around the world.

At the core of Bossa Nova lies the pulsating rhythms of the samba, the quintessential Brazilian dance music that had long been a fixture of the nation's cultural landscape. Drawing upon the infectious, syncopated beats and the emotive, poetic lyrics of the samba tradition, the pioneering Bossa Nova musicians sought to create a more understated, refined, and introspective musical form that would come to embody the laid-back, sophisticated sensibilities of the emerging Brazilian middle class.

Alongside the samba influence, Bossa Nova also owes a significant debt to the rich legacy of Brazilian jazz, a genre that had been steadily gaining popularity and critical acclaim on the international stage. The Bossa Nova artists, inspired by the harmonic complexity and expressive potential of jazz, sought to seamlessly integrate these elements into the rhythmic foundation of the samba, creating a captivating hybrid that blended the two musical traditions into a cohesive and captivating whole.

Moreover, the distinctive melancholic and poetic qualities that have become hallmarks of the Bossa Nova sound can be traced back to the enduring influence of the traditional Brazilian ballads and folk songs that had long been a part of the nation's cultural heritage.

The Bossa Nova practitioners, in their quest to craft a musical form that would resonate with the changing social and cultural landscape of Brazil, drew upon these lyrical and melodic traditions, imbuing their compositions with a sense of introspection and a profound emotional resonance.

The confluence of these diverse musical influences – the rhythmic vitality of the samba, the harmonic sophistication of Brazilian jazz, and the melancholic sensibilities of the nation's folk traditions – gave rise to the distinctive sound and captivating essence of Bossa Nova. As this genre gained popularity and critical acclaim within Brazil, it began to captivate audiences around the world, paving the way for its remarkable cross-cultural dissemination and the profound impact it would have on the musical traditions of Portugal.

The deep-rooted cultural and linguistic ties that bind Brazil and Portugal have long served as a conduit for the exchange of artistic and musical traditions, a dynamic interplay that has profoundly shaped the evolution of both nations' cultural landscapes. It is within this context of cross-cultural fertilization that the remarkable influence of Bossa Nova on the musical traditions of Portugal can be understood.

The historical and linguistic connections between Brazil and Portugal, forged through centuries of colonial rule and the shared legacy of the Portuguese language, have fostered a cultural kinship that has manifested in the realm of music. As Bossa Nova gained international recognition and acclaim, Portuguese artists and audiences were quick to embrace the genre, recognizing in its captivating melodies and rhythmic sensibilities a resonance with their own cultural heritage and musical traditions.

One of the key factors that facilitated the seamless integration of Bossa Nova into the Portuguese musical landscape was the deeply rooted presence of the Portuguese guitar, an instrument that had long been a fixture of the nation's enduring musical legacy. The distinctive sound and expressive capabilities of the Portuguese guitar, with its twelve-string configuration and its ability to blend soulful melodies with intricate rhythmic patterns, found a natural synergy with the nuanced harmonies and understated grooves of Bossa Nova.

As Portuguese musicians began to explore and experiment with the Bossa Nova genre, they found within its musical framework a platform for the expression of their own cultural and artistic identities. The melancholic sensibilities and poetic lyricism that had long been hallmarks of traditional Portuguese music found a natural complement in the introspective and emotionally resonant qualities of Bossa Nova, creating a vibrant and captivating musical fusion that would come to define the evolution of Portuguese music in the latter half of the 20th century.

Moreover, the cross-pollination of musical styles between Brazil and Portugal was not a one-way street; the influence flowed in both directions, with Portuguese artists and composers contributing their unique artistic voices and musical traditions to the Bossa Nova canon. This dynamic exchange not only enriched the genre's sonic palette but also served to forge a deeper, more profound cultural connection between the two Lusophone nations, solidifying their status as partners in the ongoing evolution of global music.

As the captivating sound of Bossa Nova permeated the musical consciousness of Portugal, the nation's artists and audiences embraced the genre with a fervor that would forever alter the trajectory of the country's musical landscape. From the intimate Fado houses of Lisbon to the concert halls and recording studios across the nation, Bossa Nova found a receptive and enthusiastic home, sparking a remarkable creative renaissance that would leave an indelible mark on the Portuguese musical tradition.

One of the key factors that contributed to the widespread popularity and adaptation of Bossa Nova in Portugal was the genre's natural affinity with the nation's enduring musical legacy, particularly the Fado tradition. The emotive, introspective qualities of Bossa Nova, combined with its seamless integration of the Portuguese guitar, allowed Portuguese musicians to seamlessly weave the Brazilian genre into the fabric of their cultural heritage, creating a captivating and wholly unique musical synthesis.

The pioneering work of artists such as Amália Rodrigues and José Afonso, who were among the first to explore the creative potential of blending Bossa Nova with traditional Portuguese music, catalyzed the genre's widespread acceptance and dissemination. Through their dynamic and innovative interpretations, these musicians demonstrated the remarkable versatility of Bossa Nova, showcasing its ability to enhance and enrich the enduring musical traditions of Portugal.

As the popularity of Bossa Nova continued to grow within Portugal, the nation's artists began to push the boundaries of the genre, infusing it with their unique stylistic influences and artistic visions. The emergence of a new generation of musicians, such as Sérgio Godinho and Rui

Veloso, who drew upon the Bossa Nova aesthetic while incorporating elements of rock, jazz, and the nation's folk traditions, further expanded the genre's creative possibilities and cemented its status as a vital component of the Portuguese musical landscape.

The adaptation and popularization of Bossa Nova in Portugal were not limited to the realm of music; the genre's captivating visual aesthetic and its association with the sophisticated, urbane sensibilities of the Brazilian middle class also found a receptive audience within the nation's cultural sphere. The iconic imagery and design elements associated with Bossa Nova, from the album covers to the fashions and lifestyle aesthetics, were eagerly embraced by the Portuguese creative community, further reinforcing the genre's status as a symbol of cosmopolitan cool and artistic innovation.

The remarkable dissemination and adaptation of Bossa Nova within the Portuguese musical landscape have had a profound and lasting impact, serving as a testament to the power of cross-cultural exchange and the enduring capacity of music to transcend geographic and linguistic boundaries. The seamless integration of the Brazilian genre into the rich tapestry of Portuguese musical traditions has not only enriched the nation's cultural heritage but has also positioned Portugal as a vital hub of global musical innovation and artistic collaboration.

As the captivating sound of Bossa Nova continues to resonate within the musical consciousness of Portugal, its enduring legacy has become a testament to the transformative power of cross-cultural exchange and the remarkable ability of music to forge enduring connections between nations and peoples.

The influence of Bossa Nova on the evolution of Portuguese music has been profound and far-reaching, manifesting in the work of successive generations of artists who have drawn upon the genre's distinctive sonic and emotional qualities to create captivating new forms of musical expression. From the seamless integration of Bossa Nova into the Fado tradition to the experimental fusion of the genre with the nation's rich folk and rock influences, the Portuguese musical landscape has been indelibly shaped by the Brazilian genre's enduring presence.

Moreover, the legacy of Bossa Nova in Portugal extends beyond the realm of music, serving as a powerful symbol of the cultural and artistic kinship that binds the two Lusophone nations. The widespread embrace and adaptation of the Brazilian genre within the

Portuguese cultural sphere have solidified the nation's status as a vital hub of global musical innovation, a place where the artistic traditions of diverse cultures converge and cross-pollinate to create captivating new forms of expression.

The enduring impact of Bossa Nova on the Portuguese musical landscape can also be seen in how the genre has catalyzed the exploration and celebration of the nation's rich musical heritage. As Portuguese artists have incorporated elements of Bossa Nova into their work, they have also rediscovered and reinvigorated the traditional forms and styles that have long been a part of the nation's cultural identity, creating a vibrant and ever-evolving tapestry of sound that draws upon the best of both worlds.

As the world continues to grapple with the challenges of globalization and the homogenization of cultural traditions, the enduring legacy of Bossa Nova in Portugal stands as a testament to the power of music to foster cross-cultural understanding and artistic innovation. Through the seamless integration of the Brazilian genre into the nation's musical fabric, Portugal has demonstrated the remarkable capacity of music to transcend geographic and linguistic boundaries, creating a dynamic and ever-evolving cultural landscape that continues to inspire and captivate audiences around the world.

Among the contemporary Bossa Nova artists who have emerged as the custodians of this captivating genre's enduring legacy in Portugal is the esteemed Susana Travassos. A classically trained musician with a deep affinity for the nuanced harmonies and emotive lyricism of Bossa Nova, Travassos has become renowned for her ability to blend the traditional elements of the genre with her distinctive interpretive approach.

Travassos' captivating performances are a

testament to her mastery of the Portuguese guitar, the hallmark instrument that has long been synonymous with the Bossa Nova tradition in Portugal. Through her deft and delicate manipulation of the instrument's twelve-string configuration, she can coax from it a rich, resonant sound that serves as the foundation for her emotive vocal deliveries and intricate harmonic explorations.

Moreover, Travassos' artistic vision is deeply rooted in the preservation and evolution of the Bossa Nova tradition, as evidenced by her meticulous attention to the genre's historical context and her unwavering commitment to honoring the distinctive stylistic and thematic elements that have long defined the genre. From the seamless integration of traditional Portuguese musical motifs to the exploration of the poetic narratives that have become the hallmark of Bossa Nova, Travassos' work consistently demonstrates a profound reverence for the genre's enduring legacy.

Yet, Travassos' contribution to the contemporary Bossa Nova landscape in Portugal extends far beyond her captivating performances. As a dedicated educator and mentor, she has played a pivotal role in fostering the next generation of Bossa Nova practitioners, imparting to them the technical mastery and creative vision that have become the hallmarks of her artistic practice. Through her tireless efforts to share her knowledge and inspire the musical aspirations of others, Travassos has cemented her status as a vital custodian of the Bossa Nova tradition, ensuring that the captivating sound of this genre will continue to resonate for generations to come.

Another remarkable contemporary Bossa Nova artist who has emerged as a guardian of the genre's enduring legacy in Portugal is the acclaimed Dulce Pontes. Known for her rich, velvety vocals and her ability to imbue the Bossa Nova form with a profound sense of emotional resonance, Pontes has become a revered figure within the nation's musical landscape, captivating audiences with her dynamic and introspective interpretations of the genre.

Like Travassos, Pontes' artistic vision is deeply rooted in the preservation and evolution of Bossa Nova, as evidenced by her meticulous attention to the genre's historical context and her unwavering commitment to honoring the distinctive stylistic and thematic elements that have long defined the form. Through her captivating performances, which seamlessly blend the understated grooves and nuanced harmonies of Bossa Nova with her own emotive and poetic sensibilities, Pontes has become a torchbearer for the genre's enduring relevance and artistic significance.

Moreover, Pontes' impact on the contemporary Bossa Nova scene in Portugal extends beyond her musical output, as she has become a tireless advocate for the genre's continued dissemination and appreciation. Through her work as a mentor and educator, she has played a pivotal role in nurturing the next generation of Bossa Nova practitioners, sharing her knowledge and expertise to ensure that the captivating sound of this genre will continue to resonate within the nation's musical consciousness.

Alongside the esteemed guardians of the Bossa Nova tradition in Portugal, a new generation of artists has emerged, poised to push the boundaries of the genre and explore its creative potential in bold and innovative ways. These remarkable musicians, drawing upon the rich legacy of their predecessors while embracing cutting-edge techniques and genre-blending approaches, have become the vanguard of a Bossa Nova renaissance that is captivating audiences both within and beyond the borders of the Iberian nation.

One such artist who has emerged as a true innovator within the contemporary Bossa Nova landscape in Portugal is the acclaimed Diogo

Clemente. A multi-instrumentalist and producer with a keen ear for sonic experimentation, Clemente has become renowned for his ability to seamlessly integrate the distinctive rhythmic and harmonic elements of Bossa Nova with a diverse array of global musical influences, from electronica to world music.

Through his dynamic and captivating recordings, Clemente has demonstrated a remarkable capacity for creative innovation, crafting Bossa Nova-inspired compositions that are simultaneously rooted in tradition and boldly forward-thinking. By incorporating elements of cutting-edge production techniques, unconventional chord voicings, and unexpected instrumental combinations, Clemente has breathed new life into the Bossa Nova genre, inspiring audiences and fellow musicians alike to expand their conception of what is possible within this captivating musical form.

Moreover, Clemente's impact on the contemporary Bossa Nova scene in Portugal extends beyond his artistic output, as he has become a tireless champion of the genre's continued evolution and global dissemination. Through his work as a producer, collaborator, and mentor, he has played a vital role in fostering a vibrant and dynamic ecosystem of Bossa Nova practitioners, inspiring them to push the boundaries of the genre and explore its creative potential in bold and innovative ways.

Another remarkable artist who has emerged as a leading innovator within the contemporary Bossa Nova landscape in Portugal is the acclaimed Catarina Pires. A vocalist and multi-instrumentalist with a deep affinity for the genre's nuanced harmonies and emotive lyricism, Pires has become renowned for her ability to seamlessly blend the traditional elements of Bossa Nova with a diverse array of global musical influences, from jazz to world music.

Through her captivating performances and meticulously crafted recordings, Pires has demonstrated a remarkable capacity for creative innovation, crafting Bossa Nova-inspired compositions that are simultaneously rooted in tradition and boldly experimental. By incorporating elements of cutting-edge production techniques, unconventional vocal stylings, and unexpected instrumental combinations, Pires has breathed new life into the Bossa Nova genre, inspiring audiences and fellow musicians alike to expand their conception of what is possible within this captivating musical form.

Moreover, Pires' impact on the contemporary

Bossa Nova scene in Portugal extends beyond her artistic output, as she has become a tireless advocate for the genre's continued evolution and global dissemination. Through her work as a mentor, educator, and collaborator, she has played a vital role in fostering a vibrant and dynamic ecosystem of Bossa Nova practitioners, inspiring them to push the boundaries of the genre and explore its creative potential in bold and innovative ways.

As the contemporary Bossa Nova landscape in Portugal continues to evolve and diversify, a cohort of remarkable artists has emerged, poised to shape the future trajectory of this captivating musical form. These visionary musicians, drawing upon the rich legacy of their predecessors while embracing cutting-edge technologies, experimental approaches, and bold creative visions, have become the vanguard of a Bossa Nova renaissance that is captivating audiences both within and beyond the borders of the Iberian nation.

One such visionary is the acclaimed Júlio Resende, a pianist and composer whose innovative and genre-defying approach to Bossa Nova has earned him widespread critical acclaim and a devoted following among audiences and fellow musicians alike. Through his dynamic and captivating recordings,

Resende has demonstrated a remarkable capacity for creative synthesis, seamlessly blending the distinctive rhythmic and harmonic elements of Bossa Nova with a diverse array of global musical influences, from classical and jazz to electronic and world music.

At the heart of Resende's artistic vision is a deep-rooted commitment to innovation and the exploration of new creative frontiers. By incorporating cutting-edge production techniques, unconventional chord voicings, and unexpected instrumental combinations, he has crafted a distinctly modern and forward-thinking interpretation of Bossa Nova that has the power to captivate and inspire audiences across the spectrum of musical tastes.

Moreover, Resende's impact on the contemporary Bossa Nova scene in Portugal extends far beyond his remarkable artistic output. Through his work as a mentor, educator, and collaborative visionary, he has become a driving force behind the ongoing evolution and dissemination of the genre, nurturing the next generation of Bossa Nova practitioners and inspiring them to push the boundaries of what is possible within this captivating musical form.

Another visionary whose work has had a

profound impact on the contemporary Bossa Nova landscape in Portugal is the acclaimed Filipe Melo. A multi-talented musician, composer, and producer, Melo has become renowned for his ability to seamlessly blend the traditional elements of Bossa Nova with cutting-edge electronic production techniques, creating a sonic tapestry that is both deeply rooted in the genre's enduring legacy and boldly forward-thinking.

Through his dynamic and genre-defying recordings, Melo has demonstrated a remarkable capacity for creative synthesis, effortlessly blending the lush, nuanced harmonies and emotive lyricism of Bossa Nova with the pulsating rhythms and atmospheric textures of contemporary electronic music. By embracing the creative potential of technology and digital production, Melo has breathed new life into the Bossa Nova genre, inspiring audiences and fellow musicians alike to expand their conception of what is possible within this captivating musical form.

Moreover, Melo's impact on the contemporary Bossa Nova scene in Portugal extends far beyond his artistic output, as he has become a tireless advocate for the continued evolution and global dissemination of the genre. Through his work as a mentor, collaborator, and creative visionary, he has played a pivotal role in fostering a vibrant and dynamic ecosystem of Bossa Nova practitioners, inspiring them to embrace cutting-edge technologies, experimental approaches, and bold creative visions in their pursuit of musical innovation and artistic expression.

The Bossa Nova Visionaries, represented by the remarkable talents of Júlio Resende and Filipe Melo, stand as shining examples of the remarkable ways in which the contemporary Bossa Nova landscape in Portugal is evolving and diversifying. By embracing the enduring legacy of the genre while simultaneously pushing the boundaries of what is possible within its sonic and thematic parameters, these visionary artists have become the torchbearers of a Bossa Nova renaissance that is captivating audiences and inspiring fellow musicians both within and beyond the borders of the Iberian nation.

As we delve into the vibrant tapestry of contemporary Bossa Nova artists in Portugal, we are confronted with the remarkable ways in which this captivating musical genre has continued to evolve and adapt, serving as a vital and enduring component of the nation's cultural landscape. From the esteemed guardians of the tradition to the innovative experimentalists and visionary pioneers, the Bossa Nova practitioners of modern-day

Portugal have demonstrated a remarkable capacity for creative expression, technical mastery, and the preservation of a legacy that extends far beyond the boundaries of the Iberian Peninsula.

The enduring resonance of Bossa Nova within the Portuguese musical consciousness is a testament to the remarkable power of music to transcend geographic and linguistic barriers, forging deep and lasting connections between diverse cultures and peoples. As the contemporary Bossa Nova artists of Portugal have continued to captivate and inspire audiences around the world, they have become the living embodiments of a tradition that has long been regarded as a universal language of artistic expression.

Moreover, the remarkable diversity and innovation that have come to define the contemporary Bossa Nova landscape in Portugal serve as a testament to the remarkable resilience and adaptability of the genre itself. As the artists have embraced cutting-edge technologies, experimental approaches, and bold creative visions, they have demonstrated the remarkable capacity of Bossa Nova to evolve and thrive in the face of a rapidly changing cultural landscape, cementing its status as a vital and enduring component of the global musical tapestry.

The enduring resonance of Bossa Nova in Portugal is not merely a reflection of the genre's artistic merit; it is also a testament to the deep-rooted cultural connections and shared artistic sensibilities that have long bound the Lusophone nations together. As the contemporary Bossa Nova practitioners of Portugal have continued to forge cross-cultural collaborations and creative exchanges with their counterparts in Brazil and beyond, they have become the living embodiments of a musical tradition that serves as a powerful conduit for the expression of the human experience in all its complex and nuanced glory.

The story of contemporary Bossa Nova artists in Portugal is not merely a tale of musical innovation and technical mastery; it is a narrative of the enduring power of art to shape and reflect the collective identity of a nation, to forge connections between diverse cultures, and to inspire the ongoing evolution of global culture. As these remarkable musicians continue to captivate and inspire audiences around the world, they stand as shining examples of the transformative potential of music to transcend the boundaries of time and space and to shape the very fabric of the human experience.

FOLK MUSIC

In the verdant and picturesque northern region of Minho, the captivating world of Portuguese folk music is defined by the haunting and ethereal melodies that have long been the hallmark of the region's cultural heritage. Drawing upon a rich tapestry of historical influences, from the Galician-Portuguese ballads of the medieval era to the soulful laments of the Iberian Peninsula's

Moorish inhabitants, the folk music traditions of Minho have evolved into a captivating and multifaceted tapestry of sound that continues to captivate audiences both within and beyond the borders of Portugal.

At the heart of the Minho folk music tradition lies the distinctive sound of the Concertina, a compact and versatile accordion-like instrument that has become synonymous with the region's musical identity. The Concertina, with its rich, resonant tone and its ability to seamlessly blend expressive melodies with intricate rhythmic accompaniment, has long been the cornerstone of Minho's folk music, serving as the foundation for the region's captivating vocal traditions and the spirited dance forms that have become integral to its cultural celebrations.

Moreover, the Concertina is not the only instrumental stalwart of the Minho folk music tradition; the region is also renowned for its skilled practitioners of the Bagpipe, a traditional wind instrument that has deep roots in the Iberian Peninsula's Celtic heritage. The haunting, ethereal sound of the Minho Bagpipe, with its distinctive drone and the plaintive melodies that it is capable of producing, has become a vital component of the region's musical tapestry, lending an air of mysticism and timelessness to the folk traditions that have been passed down through the generations.

The vocal traditions of the Minho region, too, are a remarkable and captivating aspect of its folk music heritage. From the soulful lamentations of the Cantigas de Amigo, which draw upon the region's history of Galician-Portuguese poetic expression, to the spirited call-and-response chants that have become integral to the region's festive celebrations, the voices of Minho's folk musicians have the power to captivate and transport the listener to a realm of profound emotional resonance.

As the folk music traditions of the Minho region

have continued to evolve and adapt to the changing tides of the modern world, the remarkable resilience and adaptability of these artistic forms have become increasingly apparent. Through the tireless efforts of preservationists and revivalists, the distinctive sounds and cultural practices of Minho's folk music have been safeguarded and reinvigorated, ensuring that this precious legacy will continue to resonate with audiences for generations to come.

In the vast and enchanting expanse of the Alentejo region, the heartbeat of Portuguese folk music is defined by a spirited and infectious rhythmic pulse that has long been the hallmark of the area's cultural identity. Drawing upon a rich tapestry of historical influences, from the ancient Moorish and Roman traditions that have left an indelible mark on the region's artistic sensibilities to the vibrant Iberian folk music styles that have flourished in the area for centuries, the folk music of Alentejo is a captivating and multifaceted tapestry of sound that continues to captivate audiences both within and beyond the borders of Portugal.

At the core of the Alentejo folk music tradition lies the distinctive sound of the Viola Campaniça, a plucked string instrument that has become synonymous with the region's musical identity. With its rich, resonant tone and its ability to seamlessly blend expressive melodies with intricate rhythmic accompaniment, the Viola Campaniça has long been the cornerstone of Alentejo's folk music, serving as the foundation for the region's spirited vocal traditions and the lively dance forms that have become integral to its cultural celebrations.

Alongside the Viola Campaniça, the Alentejo folk music tradition is also renowned for its skilled practitioners of the Adufe, a traditional frame drum that has deep roots in the Iberian Peninsula's Moorish heritage. The powerful, percussive sound of the Adufe, with its distinctive rhythmic patterns and its ability to infuse the music with a sense of infectious energy, has become a vital component of the Alentejo folk music tapestry, lending an air of vitality and celebration to the region's cultural traditions.

The vocal traditions of the Alentejo region, too, are a remarkable and captivating aspect of its folk music heritage. From the soulful and introspective Cante Alentejano, a style of polyphonic singing that has been recognized as an Intangible Cultural Heritage of Humanity by UNESCO, to the spirited call-and-response chants that have become integral to the region's festive celebrations, the voices of Alentejo's folk musicians have the power to captivate and inspire audiences, imbuing the music with a profound sense of emotional resonance and cultural identity.

As the folk music traditions of the Alentejo region have continued to evolve and adapt to the changing tides of the modern world, the remarkable resilience and adaptability of these artistic forms have become increasingly apparent. Through the tireless efforts of preservationists and revivalists, the distinctive sounds and cultural practices of Alentejo's folk music have been safeguarded and reinvigorated, ensuring that this precious legacy will continue to resonate with audiences for generations to come.

In the far-flung archipelago of the Azores, the captivating world of Portuguese folk music is defined by a melodic tapestry that reflects the region's unique history, geography, and cultural heritage. Drawing upon a rich blend of continental Portuguese, Moorish, and New World influences, the folk music traditions of the Azores have evolved into a captivating and multifaceted tapestry of sound that continues to captivate audiences both within and beyond the borders of Portugal.

At the heart of the Azores folk music tradition lies the distinctive sound of the Viola da Terra, a plucked string instrument that has become synonymous with the region's musical identity. With its rich, resonant tone and its ability to seamlessly blend expressive melodies with intricate rhythmic accompaniment, the Viola da Terra has long been the cornerstone of the Azores' folk music, serving as the foundation for the region's lyrical vocal traditions and the spirited dance forms that have become integral to its cultural celebrations.

Alongside the Viola da Terra, the Azores folk music tradition is also renowned for its skilled practitioners of the Cavaquinho, a diminutive four-string instrument that has deep roots in the Iberian Peninsula's Moorish and Brazilian musical traditions. The bright, nimble sound of the Cavaquinho, combined with its ability to infuse the music with a sense of infectious energy and rhythmic vitality, has become a vital component of the Azores folk music tapestry, lending a unique and captivating dimension to the region's cultural traditions.

The vocal traditions of the Azores, too, are a remarkable and captivating aspect of its folk music heritage. From the soulful and introspective Cantigas de Trabalho, which draw upon the region's history of agricultural labor and maritime pursuits, to the spirited and celebratory Ranchos Folclóricos, which blend traditional dance forms with rousing vocal performances, the voices of the Azores' folk musicians have the power to captivate and transport the listener to a realm of profound emotional resonance and cultural significance.

As the folk music traditions of the Azores have continued to evolve and adapt to the changing tides of the modern world, the remarkable resilience and adaptability of these artistic forms have become increasingly apparent. Through the tireless efforts of preservationists and revivalists, the distinctive sounds and cultural practices of the Azores' folk music have been safeguarded and reinvigorated, ensuring that this precious legacy will continue to resonate with audiences for generations to come.

At the very heart of the vibrant and multifaceted world of Portuguese regional folk music lies a captivating tapestry of festivals and cultural celebrations that serve as the lifeblood of these enduring artistic traditions. From the spirited and colorful festivities of the Minho region to the soulful and introspective observances of the Alentejo, these vibrant gatherings are not merely events of entertainment; they are vital and irreplaceable components of the nation's cultural identity, serving as the conduits through which the rich legacy of Portuguese folk music is preserved, celebrated, and passed down through the generations.

One of the most renowned and captivating festivals in the Portuguese folk music landscape is the Festa dos Tabuleiros, a biennial celebration that takes place in the historic city of Tomar in the Ribatejo region. This remarkable event, which dates back to the 16th century, is a dazzling display of the region's folk music traditions, with spirited performances of traditional songs and dances, the parading of elaborately decorated "tabuleiros" (trays), and the participation of costumed revelers who embody the cultural heritage of the area.

The Festa dos Tabuleiros is not merely a celebration of the region's folk music; it is also a testament to the remarkable resilience and adaptability of these artistic traditions. Over the centuries, the festival has evolved and adapted to the changing tides of Portuguese society, incorporating new influences and techniques while maintaining a steadfast allegiance to the core cultural essence that has defined the Ribatejo's musical heritage for generations.

Another remarkable festival that serves as a vital celebration of Portuguese folk music is the Festival de Paredes de Coura, an annual event that takes place in the Minho region and is renowned for its diverse and captivating lineup of performers. From the haunting melodies of traditional Minho ballads to the spirited and infectious rhythms of contemporary folk-inspired acts, this festival has become a hub for the preservation, dissemination, and evolution of the nation's regional musical traditions, drawing audiences from across Portugal and beyond.

The Festival de Paredes de Coura is not merely a showcase of musical talent; it is also a testament to the deep-rooted connections that bind the diverse communities of the Minho region together. Through the shared experience of these vibrant celebrations, the festival serves as a conduit for the expression of regional identity, fostering a sense of cultural unity and pride that resonates far beyond the confines of the event itself.

In the Alentejo region, the remarkable Festa da Flor, an annual celebration that takes place in the charming town of Castelo de Vide, stands as a testament to the enduring power of Portuguese folk music to shape and reflect the cultural identity of a community. This captivating festival, which features spirited performances of traditional songs and dances, the elaborately decorated "flores" (flowers) that are carried in procession, and the participation of costumed revelers who embody the region's rich cultural heritage, is a true celebration of the Alentejo's enduring musical legacy.

The Festa da Flor is not merely a festival; it is a living, breathing embodiment of the Alentejo's cultural identity, a tapestry of traditions that has been woven into the very fabric of the region's collective consciousness. Through the shared experience of these vibrant celebrations, the festival serves as a vital link between the past and the present, ensuring that the rich musical heritage of the Alentejo will continue to resonate with audiences for generations to come.

These captivating festivals and cultural celebrations, which serve as the heartbeat of Portuguese regional folk music, are not merely events of entertainment; they are vital and irreplaceable components of the nation's cultural identity, preserving and disseminating the rich legacy of these artistic traditions while simultaneously serving as platforms for the exploration and evolution of new musical forms. Through the shared experience of these vibrant gatherings, the diverse communities of Portugal can come together, celebrate their cultural heritage, and forge a deeper, more profound connection to the enduring power of music to shape and reflect the human experience.

As we delve into the rich tapestry of Portuguese regional folk music, we are confronted with the remarkable resilience and adaptability of these artistic traditions, which have continued to captivate and inspire audiences both within and beyond the borders of the Iberian nation. From the haunting melodies of the Minho region to the spirited rhythms of the Alentejo, and the captivating melodic tapestry of the Azores, the diverse musical forms that have flourished across Portugal's diverse landscape serve as a testament to the enduring power of art to shape and reflect the collective identity of a people.

At the heart of this remarkable legacy lies the profound connection between these regional folk music traditions and the cultural identity of the communities that have nurtured and preserved them over the centuries. Whether it is the deep-rooted reverence for the Concertina in Minho, the spirited celebration of the Viola Campaniça in the Alentejo, or the captivating interplay of the Viola da Terra and Cavaquinho in the Azores, these distinctive instruments and the musical styles they embody have become inextricably linked with the very essence of the regions they represent.

Moreover, the enduring legacy of Portuguese regional folk music extends far beyond the realm of mere artistic expression; it is a vital component of the nation's cultural heritage, serving as a conduit for the preservation and dissemination of the diverse histories, customs, and artistic sensibilities that have long defined the Portuguese experience. Through the tireless efforts of preservationists, revivalists, and the communities that continue to embrace and celebrate these musical traditions, the rich legacy of Portuguese folk music has been safeguarded and reinvigorated, ensuring that it will continue to resonate with audiences for generations to come.

The remarkable diversity and adaptability of these regional folk music traditions have also played a vital role in the ongoing evolution of Portuguese music as a whole. As contemporary artists and musicians have continued to explore and incorporate elements of these enduring styles into their creative endeavors, the regional folk music of Portugal has become a vital wellspring of inspiration and innovation, catalyzing the development of new and captivating musical forms that continue to captivate audiences across the globe.

The enduring legacy of Portuguese regional folk music is not merely a testament to the remarkable artistry and technical mastery of the musicians who have dedicated their lives to these traditions; it is a reflection of the profound cultural, historical, and emotional connections that have long defined the Portuguese experience. Through the shared experience of these vibrant musical forms, the diverse communities of the Iberian nation have been able to come together, celebrate their heritage, and forge a deeper, more profound understanding of the enduring power of art to shape and reflect the human experience.

FUSIONS AND INNOVATIONS

In the enthralling domain of Portuguese music, a fresh cohort of artists has arisen, ready to expand the limits of conventional forms and styles by skillfully fusing an array of musical inspirations and innovative production methods. These remarkable musicians, drawing upon the rich legacy of their nation's musical heritage while embracing bold and innovative approaches, have become the vanguard of a cultural renaissance that is captivating audiences both within and beyond the borders of the Iberian Peninsula.

One such artist who has emerged as a true trailblazer in the realm of musical fusion and innovation is the acclaimed Tiago Bettencourt. A multi-talented musician and producer with a deep affinity for the emotive and poetic qualities of traditional Portuguese music, Bettencourt has become renowned for his ability to seamlessly blend the distinctive sonic signatures of Fado, Alentejo folk, and contemporary rock and electronic idioms, creating a captivating sonic tapestry that is both deeply rooted in tradition and boldly forward-thinking.

Through his dynamic and genre-defying recordings, Bettencourt has demonstrated a remarkable capacity for creative synthesis, effortlessly weaving the haunting melodies and intricate guitar work of Portugal's musical heritage with the pulsating rhythms and atmospheric textures of the modern musical landscape. By embracing cutting-edge production techniques and a willingness to explore uncharted creative territories, Bettencourt has breathed new life into the very essence of Portuguese music, inspiring audiences and fellow musicians alike to expand their conception of what is possible within this captivating artistic tradition.

Alongside Bettencourt, another remarkable artist who has emerged as a pioneer of fusion and innovation within the Portuguese music scene is the acclaimed Maria Ana Bobone. A classically trained pianist with a deep fascination for the interplay of traditional and contemporary musical forms, Bobone has become renowned for her ability to seamlessly blend the emotive and introspective qualities of the Fado tradition with the harmonic sophistication and rhythmic complexity of jazz and classical music.

Through her captivating and genre-bending performances, Bobone has demonstrated a remarkable capacity for creative reimagination, crafting compositions that serve as a testament to the enduring vitality and evolution of Portuguese music. By embracing the expressive potential of the piano as a conduit for the exploration of her nation's musical heritage, Bobone has become a driving force behind the continued reinvention and revitalization of traditional Portuguese genres, inspiring audiences and fellow musicians alike to expand their conception of what is possible within this captivating artistic tradition.

Bettencourt and Maria Ana Bobone are but two

examples of the remarkable ways in which the contemporary Portuguese music landscape has continued to evolve and adapt to the changing tides of the global cultural landscape. Through the seamless integration of traditional forms with cutting-edge production techniques, bold experimentation, and a deep-rooted commitment to the preservation and evolution of their nation's musical heritage, these remarkable artists have become the torchbearers of a cultural renaissance that is captivating audiences both within and beyond the borders of Portugal.

At the heart of the remarkable metamorphosis that has continued to shape the contemporary

Portuguese music landscape lies a profound and enduring dedication to the exploration of cross-cultural connections and the forging of unprecedented artistic collaborations. As the nation's musicians have continued to look beyond the borders of the Iberian Peninsula, they have embraced the remarkable diversity of global musical traditions, weaving them into the very fabric of their creative endeavors and, in the process, expanding the horizons of what is possible within the realm of Portuguese music.

One such remarkable collaboration that has captured the imagination of audiences around the world is the dynamic partnership between the acclaimed Portuguese artist Mariza and the legendary Senegalese singer Youssou N'Dour. Drawing upon the emotive and poetic qualities of the Fado tradition and the rhythmic vitality of West African musical forms, this captivating cross-cultural exchange has resulted in a series of dynamic and genre-defying recordings that have served to blur the boundaries between musical traditions and to forge a profound and enduring connection between the diverse cultures of the Lusophone and Francophone worlds.

Through their seamless integration of the distinctive vocal styles, instrumentation, and thematic sensibilities that define their respective musical traditions, Mariza and

Youssou N'Dour have demonstrated the remarkable capacity of music to transcend linguistic and geographical barriers, serving as a powerful conduit for the expression of shared human experiences and the fostering of deeper cross-cultural understanding. By embracing the creative potential of collaborative artistic endeavors, these remarkable musicians have not only captivated audiences with their innovative and genre-bending explorations but have also played a vital role in shaping the future trajectory of Portuguese music as a whole.

Another remarkable cross-cultural collaboration that has left an indelible mark on the contemporary Portuguese music landscape is the dynamic partnership between the acclaimed Angolan artist Bonga and the renowned Portuguese musician Rodrigo Leão. Drawing upon the rich musical heritage of the Lusophone world, this captivating exchange has resulted in a series of recordings that seamlessly blend the distinctive rhythms and vocal styles of Angolan music with the emotive and introspective qualities of the Portuguese tradition, creating a sonic tapestry that is at once deeply rooted in the past and boldly forward-thinking.

Through their collaborative efforts, Bonga and Rodrigo Leão have not only captivated audiences with their innovative and genre-defying explorations but have also played a vital role in forging deeper connections between the diverse cultural and musical traditions of the Lusophone world. By embracing the creative potential of cross-cultural exchange, these remarkable artists have demonstrated the remarkable capacity of music to serve as a powerful conduit for the expression of shared experiences and the fostering of deeper intercultural understanding.

The remarkable cross-cultural collaborations that have continued to shape the contemporary Portuguese music landscape are not merely the result of individual artistic vision and technical mastery; they are also a testament to the enduring power of music to serve as a unifying force in an increasingly interconnected world. Through the seamless integration of diverse musical traditions and the forging of unprecedented global connections, these remarkable artists have not only captivated audiences with their innovative and genre-bending explorations but have also played a vital role in shaping the future trajectory of Portuguese music as a whole, ensuring that it will continue to resonate with audiences around the world for generations to come.

As the contemporary Portuguese music

landscape has continued to evolve and adapt to the ever-shifting tides of the global cultural landscape, a new generation of artists has emerged, poised to redefine the very essence of their nation's musical heritage through bold and innovative interpretations of time-honored forms and genres. These remarkable musicians, drawing upon the rich legacy of Portugal's musical past while embracing cutting-edge production techniques and a willingness to explore uncharted creative territories, have become the vanguard of a cultural renaissance that is captivating audiences both within and beyond the borders of the Iberian Peninsula.

One such artist who has emerged as a leading figure in the realm of modern interpretations of traditional Portuguese music is the acclaimed Cristina Branco. A vocalist with a rich and emotive delivery, Branco has become renowned for her ability to seamlessly blend the haunting melodies and poetic sensibilities of the Fado tradition with a contemporary sonic palette that draws upon elements of jazz, folk, and world music.

Through her captivating and genre-defying performances, Branco has demonstrated a remarkable capacity for creative reimagination, crafting interpretations of classic Fado compositions that serve as a testament to the enduring vitality and evolution of this hallowed musical form. By embracing the expressive potential of the voice as a conduit for the exploration of her nation's musical heritage, Branco has become a driving force behind the continued reinvention and revitalization of the Fado tradition, inspiring audiences and fellow musicians alike to expand their conception of what is possible within this captivating artistic form.

Alongside Cristina Branco, another remarkable artist who has made a significant impact on the modern interpretation of traditional Portuguese music is the acclaimed Filipa Pais. A multi-instrumentalist and composer with a deep affinity for the rhythmic and harmonic complexity of her nation's regional folk music traditions, Pais has become renowned for her ability to recast the distinctive sounds and stylistic elements of these time-honored forms within a contemporary sonic framework that draws upon elements of jazz, electronica, and world music.

Through her dynamic and genre-defying recordings, Pais has demonstrated a remarkable capacity for creative synthesis, effortlessly weaving the haunting melodies and intricate instrumentation of Portugal's regional folk traditions with the pulsating rhythms and atmospheric textures of the modern musical landscape. By embracing cutting-edge production techniques and a willingness to explore uncharted creative territories, Pais has breathed new life into the very essence of these time-honored musical forms, inspiring audiences and fellow musicians alike to expand their conception of what is possible within the realm of Portuguese traditional music.

The remarkable modern interpretations of traditional Portuguese music embodied by the work of Cristina Branco and Filipa Pais are but two examples of the remarkable ways in which the contemporary music landscape of the Iberian nation has continued to evolve and adapt to the changing tides of the global cultural landscape. Through the seamless integration of time-honored forms with cutting-edge production techniques, bold experimentation, and a deep-rooted commitment to the preservation and evolution of their nation's musical heritage, these remarkable artists have become the torchbearers of a cultural renaissance that is captivating audiences both within and beyond the borders of Portugal.

As the contemporary Portuguese music landscape has continued to evolve and diversify, a remarkable cohort of artists has emerged, poised to push the boundaries of what is possible within the realm of musical expression. These visionary musicians, drawing upon the rich legacy of their nation's musical traditions while embracing cutting-edge technologies, experimental approaches, and bold creative visions, have become the vanguard of a cultural renaissance that is captivating audiences both within and beyond the borders of the Iberian Peninsula.

One such visionary who has emerged as a leading figure in the realm of experimental Portuguese music is the acclaimed Ruben Alves. A multi-talented composer, producer, and sound artist, Alves has become renowned for his ability to seamlessly blend elements of traditional Portuguese music, contemporary electronica, and avant-garde compositional techniques, creating a sonic tapestry that is both deeply rooted in the nation's cultural heritage and boldly forward-thinking.

Through his dynamic and genre-defying recordings, Alves has demonstrated a remarkable capacity for creative synthesis, effortlessly weaving the haunting melodies and intricate instrumentation of Portugal's musical past with pulsating rhythms, atmospheric textures, and cutting-edge production techniques of the modern electronic landscape. By embracing the creative potential of digital technologies and a willingness to explore uncharted creative territories, Alves has breathed new life into the very essence of Portuguese music, inspiring audiences and fellow musicians alike to expand their conception of what is possible within this captivating artistic tradition.

Alongside Ruben Alves, another visionary whose work has had a profound impact on the experimental music landscape of contemporary Portugal is the acclaimed Luísa Sobral. A singer-songwriter with a deep affinity for the poetic nuances and emotional resonance of her nation's musical heritage, Sobral has become renowned for her ability to seamlessly blend the distinctive sonic signatures of Fado, folk, and contemporary pop, creating a captivating and genre-defying body of work that has the power to captivate and inspire audiences across the musical spectrum.

Through her dynamic and unconventional recordings, Sobral has demonstrated a remarkable capacity for creative reimagination, crafting compositions that serve as a testament to the enduring vitality and evolution of Portuguese music. By embracing the expressive potential of the singer-songwriter format as a conduit for the exploration of her nation's musical heritage, Sobral has become a driving force behind the continued reinvention and revitalization of traditional Portuguese genres, inspiring audiences and fellow musicians alike to expand their conception of what is possible within the realm of musical expression.

The remarkable experimental and genre-bending approaches embodied by the work of Ruben Alves and Luísa Sobral are but two examples of the remarkable ways in which the contemporary Portuguese music landscape has continued to evolve and diversify, pushing the boundaries of what is possible within the realm of artistic expression. Through the seamless integration of traditional forms with cutting-edge technologies, bold experimentation, and a deep-rooted commitment to the continued evolution of their nation's musical heritage, these visionary artists have become the torchbearers of a cultural renaissance that is captivating audiences both within and beyond the borders of Portugal.

As we delve into the remarkable tapestry of fusions, collaborations, modern interpretations, and experimental soundscapes that have come to define the contemporary Portuguese music landscape, we are confronted with the profound and enduring impact that these remarkable artistic endeavors have had on the nation's cultural identity and the ongoing evolution of global music as a whole.

From the dynamic fusion of traditional forms with cutting-edge production techniques to the visionary collaborations that have forged unprecedented connections between the Iberian nation and the diverse musical traditions of the world, the artists who have emerged as the trailblazers of this remarkable cultural renaissance have demonstrated a remarkable capacity for creative synthesis and a deep-rooted commitment to the continued evolution of Portuguese music.

Through their innovative and genre-defying explorations, these remarkable musicians have not only captivated audiences with their bold and boundary-pushing artistic visions but have also played a vital role in shaping the future trajectory of their nation's musical heritage. By seamlessly integrating the distinctive sonic signatures and thematic sensibilities of time-honored forms with the pulsating rhythms, atmospheric textures, and cutting-edge production techniques of the modern musical landscape, they have breathed new life into the very essence of Portuguese music, inspiring audiences and fellow artists alike to expand their conception of what is possible within this captivating artistic tradition.

Moreover, the remarkable cross-cultural collaborations that have continued to shape the contemporary Portuguese music landscape have served as a powerful testament to the enduring power of music to transcend geographic and linguistic barriers, forging deep and lasting connections between diverse cultures and peoples. Through these unprecedented artistic exchanges, the musicians of Portugal have not only captivated global audiences with their innovative and genre-bending explorations but have also played a vital role in fostering a deeper sense of intercultural understanding and the celebration of shared human experiences.

As the experimental and genre-defying approaches that have become the hallmarks of the contemporary Portuguese music scene continue to captivate and inspire audiences around the world, it is clear that the enduring legacy of these remarkable artistic endeavors will continue to reverberate long into the future. Whether through the seamless fusion of traditional forms with cutting-edge production techniques, the visionary collaborations that have forged unprecedented global connections, or the bold and boundary-pushing interpretations of time-honored musical genres, the remarkable musicians of Portugal have demonstrated a remarkable capacity for creative reinvention and a deep-rooted commitment to the continued evolution of their nation's cultural heritage.

CULTURAL IMPACT AND IDENTITY

At the very heart of the profound cultural impact and identity-shaping power of Portuguese music lies the remarkable ways in which this captivating art form has become a vital reflection of the nation's history, customs, and deeply rooted artistic sensibilities. From the haunting melodies of Fado, which have long been regarded as the quintessential embodiment of the Portuguese spirit, to the

---

spirited rhythms and distinctive regional folk traditions that serve as expressions of local cultural identities, the sonic landscape of the Iberian nation has become a powerful mirror, reflecting the multifaceted and ever-evolving narrative of the Portuguese experience.

One of the most remarkable and enduring examples of how music has become a vital reflection of Portuguese identity is the iconic genre of Fado. Emerging from the bustling streets of Lisbon in the late 18th and early 19th centuries, this captivating musical form has long been revered as the quintessential expression of the nation's collective melancholy, resilience, and deep-rooted connection to its cultural heritage. The haunting melodies, emotive vocals, and intricate guitar work that define the Fado tradition have become a vital component of the Portuguese psyche, serving as a powerful symbol of the nation's shared experiences and the enduring spirit that has sustained its people through the trials and tribulations of history.

Beyond the enduring legacy of Fado, the remarkably diverse regional folk music traditions that have flourished across the Portuguese landscape have also become vital reflections of the nation's cultural identity, serving as expressions of the unique histories, customs, and artistic sensibilities that have defined the diverse communities that comprise the Iberian nation. From the haunting melodies and distinctive instrumentation of the Minho region to the spirited rhythms and vibrant celebrations of the Alentejo, these regional folk music traditions have become vital components of the Portuguese cultural tapestry, reflecting the remarkable diversity and resilience that have long defined the nation's identity.

Moreover, the profound connection between music and Portuguese identity extends far beyond the realm of traditional and folk genres, as contemporary artists and musicians have continued to draw upon the rich legacy of their nation's musical heritage in the creation of new and innovative forms of musical expression. Whether it is the dynamic fusion of Fado with cutting-edge production techniques or the seamless integration of regional folk influences into contemporary pop and rock compositions, the music of modern-day Portugal has become a vital reflection of the nation's ongoing evolution, serving as a powerful testament to the remarkable adaptability and resilience of the Portuguese artistic spirit.

Through the remarkable ways in which music has become a vital reflection of the Portuguese experience, this captivating art form has become a powerful conduit for the articulation and preservation of the nation's cultural identity, serving as a vital link between the past and the present, and ensuring that the remarkable narrative of the Portuguese people will continue to resonate with audiences around the world for generations to come.

As the profound cultural impact and identity-shaping power of Portuguese music have continued to resonate within the nation's collective consciousness, this captivating art form has also become a vital component of the country's national and international representation, serving as a powerful ambassador for the Iberian nation's rich cultural heritage and the remarkable diversity of its artistic traditions.

One of the most remarkable examples of how Portuguese music has come to play a pivotal role in national representation can be found in the enduring legacy of Fado, which has become a vital symbol of the nation's cultural identity both within and beyond the borders of the Iberian Peninsula. The recognition of Fado as an Intangible Cultural Heritage of Humanity by UNESCO in 2011 not only served to highlight the profound cultural significance of this captivating musical genre but also positioned it as a vital component of Portugal's national brand, a captivating representation of the nation's artistic legacy that has resonated with audiences around the world.

Beyond the international recognition and acclaim afforded to the Fado tradition, the remarkable regional folk music styles that have flourished across the Portuguese landscape have also become vital components of the nation's cultural representation, serving as powerful expressions of the diverse artistic sensibilities and local identities that comprise the Iberian nation. From the haunting melodies of the Minho region to the spirited rhythms of the Alentejo, these regional folk music traditions have become captivating ambassadors for the remarkable diversity and resilience that have long defined the Portuguese cultural experience.

Moreover, the remarkable influence of contemporary Portuguese music on the global stage has also become a vital component of the nation's international representation, as a new generation of artists and musicians have continued to draw upon the rich legacy of their nation's musical heritage in the creation of innovative and genre-defying forms of artistic expression. Whether it is the dynamic fusion of traditional Portuguese genres with cutting-edge production techniques or the seamless integration of regional folk influences into captivating contemporary compositions, the music of modern-day Portugal has become a vital reflection of the nation's ongoing evolution, serving as a powerful testament to the remarkable adaptability and creative vision of its artistic community.

The remarkable ways in which Portuguese music has come to play a pivotal role in the nation's national and international representation have not only served to captivate audiences around the world but have also helped to shape perceptions of Portugal's cultural identity on the global stage. By positioning the nation's rich musical heritage as a vital component of its cultural brand, Portugal has not only fostered deeper connections with the international community but has also reinforced the remarkable resilience and adaptability of its artistic traditions, ensuring that the remarkable narrative of the Portuguese experience will continue to resonate with audiences around the world for generations to come.

In the mesmerizing world of Portuguese music, the deep-rooted cultural significance and identity-defining influence of this remarkable art form have transcended mere artistic expression and national symbolism, playing a crucial role in fueling the country's flourishing tourism sector and bolstering its strategic initiatives in the domain of cultural diplomacy.

The remarkable allure and global recognition of Portuguese music, particularly the iconic Fado tradition, have become a vital component of the nation's tourism initiatives, serving as a captivating invitation for visitors from around the world to immerse themselves in the rich cultural heritage and artistic sensibilities that have long defined the Iberian nation. From the intimate Fado houses of Lisbon to the vibrant festivals and celebrations that showcase the diverse regional folk music traditions, the musical landscape of Portugal has become a vital draw for travelers, offering a profound and immersive experience that connects them to the very essence of the Portuguese cultural identity.

Moreover, the remarkable influence of Portuguese music on the nation's tourism industry has extended far beyond the mere attraction of visitors, as the captivating sound and visual aesthetics of this remarkable art form have become vital components of the country's broader cultural branding and marketing efforts. Whether it is the iconic imagery associated with Fado performers or the distinctive regional folk music traditions that have become vital components of Portugal's tourism campaigns, the musical heritage of the Iberian nation has become a powerful tool for the articulation and dissemination of the country's cultural identity on the global stage.

Beyond the remarkable impact of Portuguese music on the nation's tourism industry, this captivating art form has also become a vital component of the country's strategic efforts in the realm of cultural diplomacy, serving as a powerful ambassador for the Iberian nation's rich cultural heritage and the remarkable diversity of its artistic traditions. Through the international dissemination and recognition of Portugal's musical legacy, the nation has not only captivated audiences around the world but has also forged deeper connections between its own cultural identity and the diverse artistic landscapes of the global community.

From the acclaimed performances of Portuguese musicians on international stages to the collaborative artistic exchanges that have transcended geographic and linguistic boundaries, the music of Portugal has become a vital tool for the nation's cultural diplomacy initiatives, fostering a deeper understanding and appreciation of the Iberian nation's remarkable artistic legacy while simultaneously positioning it as a vital hub of global cultural exchange and innovation.

The remarkable influence of Portuguese music on the nation's tourism industry and cultural diplomacy efforts is a testament to the profound and multifaceted impact of this remarkable art form, which has become a vital component of the country's collective identity and a powerful ambassador for the rich and vibrant tapestry of the Portuguese experience. As the world continues to engage with the captivating sound and visual aesthetics of Portugal's musical heritage, the nation's cultural identity and its strategic positioning on the global stage will undoubtedly continue to be shaped and reinforced by the enduring power and resonance of this remarkable artistic tradition.

As we delve into the profound cultural impact and identity-shaping power of Portuguese music, we are confronted with the remarkable ways in which this captivating art form has become woven into the very fabric of the nation's collective consciousness, serving as a vital reflection of the Iberian country's history, customs, and deeply rooted artistic sensibilities.

From the haunting melodies of Fado, which have long been revered as the quintessential embodiment of the Portuguese spirit, to the spirited rhythms and distinctive regional folk traditions that serve as expressions of local cultural identities, the musical landscape of Portugal has become a powerful mirror, reflecting the multifaceted and ever-evolving narrative of the Portuguese experience.

Moreover, the remarkable influence of Portuguese music extends far beyond the borders of the Iberian Peninsula, serving as a vital ambassador for the nation's cultural identity on the global stage. Through the international dissemination and recognition of the country's musical traditions, Portugal has not only captivated audiences around the world but has also forged deeper connections between its cultural heritage and the diverse artistic landscapes of the global community.

The profound impact of Portuguese music on the nation's tourism industry and cultural diplomacy efforts is a testament to the remarkable power and resonance of this captivating art form, which has become a vital component of the country's collective identity and a powerful invitation for the world to engage with the rich and vibrant tapestry of the Portuguese experience.

As the world continues to be captivated by the haunting melodies, spirited rhythms, and innovative explorations that define the musical traditions of Portugal, it is clear that this remarkable art form will continue to serve as a vital reflection of the nation's identity, a symphonic expression of the enduring spirit and remarkable resilience that have long defined the Portuguese experience.

Through the enduring legacy of Fado, the vibrant regional folk music traditions, and the innovative and genre-defying explorations of contemporary Portuguese artists, this captivating art form has become a vital conduit for the articulation and preservation of the nation's cultural identity, serving as a powerful testament to the remarkable adaptability and creative vision that has long characterized the Portuguese artistic spirit.

EDUCATION AND PRESERVATION

The efforts to preserve and cultivate the enduring musical legacy of Portugal lies in the vital and indispensable role of music education, a cornerstone of the nation's cultural heritage that has played a pivotal role in shaping the collective identity and artistic sensibilities of the Portuguese people.

The importance of music education in Portugal

---

can be traced back to the nation's rich history of artistic expression, where the mastery of various musical instruments and the cultivation of vocal proficiency have long been revered as vital components of a well-rounded education. From the intimate Fado houses of Lisbon to the vibrant regional folk music traditions that have flourished across the Iberian landscape, the ability to engage with and appreciate the captivating sounds of Portuguese music has been viewed as a hallmark of cultural refinement and a vital component of the nation's collective identity.

It is within this context that the remarkable network of specialized music schools, conservatories, and community-driven initiatives have emerged as the pillars of music education in Portugal, dedicated to the cultivation of musical aptitude and the preservation of the nation's enduring artistic legacy. These remarkable institutions, ranging from the prestigious Escola Superior de Música, Artes e Espetáculo in Porto to the community-based music programs that have taken root across the country, have become vital hubs of musical learning and creative expression, offering comprehensive curriculums that span the breadth of Portugal's rich musical heritage.

Moreover, the importance of music education in

Portugal extends far beyond the mere acquisition of technical proficiency; it is a vital component of the nation's broader educational system, serving as a means of cultivating a deeper appreciation for the arts, fostering creativity and self-expression, and shaping the collective identity of the Portuguese people. Through the dedicated efforts of music educators who have committed themselves to the task of nurturing the next generation of musicians, composers, and cultural ambassadors, the enduring power and resonance of Portuguese music have been woven into the very fabric of the nation's educational landscape, ensuring that this captivating art form will continue to thrive and evolve as a vital component of the Portuguese cultural experience.

The remarkable impact of music education in Portugal can be witnessed in the remarkable achievements of the nation's musicians, both past and present, who have emerged from these specialized institutions as the torchbearers of the country's enduring artistic legacy. From the iconic Fado performers who have captivated audiences around the world to the contemporary innovators who have seamlessly blended the traditional sounds of Portugal with cutting-edge musical forms, these remarkable artists have been shaped and nurtured by the robust and multifaceted music education system that has long been a hallmark of the Iberian nation.

As the world continues to grapple with the challenges of globalization and the homogenization of cultural traditions, the vital role of music education in Portugal has become increasingly crucial, serving as a bulwark against the erosion of the nation's artistic heritage and a powerful means of cultivating a deeper appreciation for the enduring power of musical expression. Through the tireless efforts of dedicated educators, the captivating sounds of Portuguese music will continue to resonate with audiences both within and beyond the borders of the Iberian Peninsula, serving as a vital reflection of the nation's collective identity and a testament to the remarkable resilience and adaptability of its cultural legacy.

Alongside the vital role of music education in shaping the cultural identity and artistic sensibilities of the Portuguese people, the remarkable efforts to preserve the nation's traditional music forms and the distinctive instruments that have long been at the heart of these captivating artistic traditions have emerged as a crucial component of the country's broader cultural preservation initiatives.

From the haunting melodies of the Fado

tradition to the spirited rhythms of the regional folk music styles that have flourished across the Iberian landscape, the musical heritage of Portugal is a tapestry woven with the distinctive sounds and deeply rooted cultural practices that have defined the nation's artistic identity for generations. It is within this context that the remarkable efforts of cultural preservationists, community advocates, and dedicated musicians have emerged as the guardians of this precious legacy, committed to ensuring that the enduring power and resonance of these captivating art forms will continue to resonate with audiences both within and beyond the borders of Portugal.

At the forefront of these preservation efforts is the remarkable work being done to safeguard the distinctive instruments that have become the sonic signatures of Portugal's traditional music forms. From the iconic Portuguese guitar, with its captivating twelve-string configuration and its pivotal role in the Fado tradition, to the regional folk instruments like the Concertina of Minho and the Viola Campaniça of the Alentejo, these remarkable tools of musical expression have become vital components of the nation's cultural heritage, imbued with the rich histories and artistic sensibilities of the communities that have nurtured them over the centuries.

The preservation of these distinctive instruments has become a crucial priority for the caretakers of Portugal's musical legacy, as they not only serve as the foundations upon which the country's traditional music forms have been built but also represent the remarkable craftsmanship and cultural significance that have long defined the Iberian nation's artistic heritage. Through the tireless efforts of skilled luthiers, the meticulous restoration and replication of these instruments, and the dedicated mentorship programs that have emerged to ensure the transference of this vital knowledge to the next generation, the enduring power and resonance of these captivating tools of musical expression have been safeguarded for the benefit of future audiences and practitioners.

Beyond the preservation of traditional instruments, the remarkable efforts to safeguard the distinctive music forms that have flourished across Portugal's diverse regional landscapes have also emerged as a vital component of the nation's cultural preservation initiatives. From the intricate and haunting Fado repertoire that has become the quintessential embodiment of the Portuguese spirit to the spirited and rhythmically complex regional folk styles that have long defined the artistic sensibilities of local communities, these captivating musical traditions have become the repositories of the nation's collective memory, imbued with the histories, customs, and artistic visions that have shaped the Portuguese experience over the centuries.

The preservation of these traditional music forms has become a multifaceted endeavor, encompassing the meticulous documentation and archiving of musical scores, the fostering of mentorship programs that ensure the transference of specialized performance techniques, and the creation of specialized festivals and cultural events that celebrate the enduring power and relevance of these captivating art forms. Through the tireless efforts of musicians, scholars, and community advocates, the remarkable diversity and enduring vitality of Portugal's traditional music have been safeguarded, ensuring that these precious cultural legacies will continue to resonate with audiences for generations to come.

As we delve into the remarkable landscape of music education and preservation efforts in Portugal, it becomes increasingly clear that these two vital components of the nation's cultural heritage are inextricably linked, each serving as a crucial pillar in the ongoing task of safeguarding the enduring power and resonance of the Iberian nation's musical legacy.

At the heart of this symbiotic relationship lies the profound role that music education has played in cultivating a deeper appreciation and understanding of the traditional music forms and distinctive instruments that have long defined the Portuguese artistic experience. Through the dedicated efforts of educators who have committed themselves to the task of nurturing the next generation of musicians, composers, and cultural ambassadors, the captivating sounds and rich histories of these precious artistic traditions have been woven into the very fabric of the nation's educational landscape, ensuring that the enduring power of Portuguese music will continue to resonate with audiences both within and beyond the borders of the Iberian Peninsula.

Moreover, the remarkable preservation efforts that have emerged to safeguard the nation's traditional music and instruments have, in turn, played a vital role in shaping the curricula and pedagogical approaches of music education institutions across Portugal. By working in close collaboration with the caretakers of these precious cultural legacies, music educators have been able to incorporate the specialized knowledge, performance techniques, and historical contexts that are essential to the perpetuation of these captivating art forms, ensuring that the next generation of Portuguese musicians will be equipped with the skills and the deep-rooted appreciation necessary to continue the remarkable tradition of musical expression that has long defined the Iberian nation.

The symbiotic relationship between music education and preservation efforts in Portugal has also manifested in the remarkable community-driven initiatives that have emerged to champion the cause of cultural heritage protection. From the grassroots efforts to restore and replicate the distinctive instruments that have become the sonic signatures of regional folk music traditions to the specialized festivals and cultural events that celebrate the enduring power of these captivating art forms, these remarkable endeavors have not only served to safeguard the nation's musical legacy but have also played a vital role in fostering a deeper appreciation and understanding of this precious cultural heritage among the Portuguese people.

As the world continues to grapple with the challenges of globalization and the homogenization of cultural traditions, the remarkable collaboration between music education and preservation efforts in Portugal has become increasingly crucial, serving as a vital bulwark against the erosion of the nation's artistic heritage and a powerful means of cultivating a deeper appreciation for the enduring power of musical expression. Through the tireless efforts of dedicated educators, cultural preservationists, and community advocates, the captivating sounds of Portuguese music will continue to resonate with audiences both within and beyond the borders of the Iberian Peninsula, serving as a vital reflection of the nation's collective identity and a testament to the remarkable resilience and adaptability of its cultural legacy.

As we delve into the remarkable landscape of music education and preservation efforts in Portugal, we are confronted with the profound and enduring impact that these vital components of the nation's cultural heritage have had on the collective identity and artistic sensibilities of the Portuguese people. From the dedicated efforts of specialized music schools and community-driven initiatives to the tireless work of cultural preservationists who have committed themselves to safeguarding the distinctive instruments and captivating music forms that have long defined the Iberian nation's artistic legacy, these remarkable endeavors have played a crucial role in shaping the enduring power and resonance of Portuguese music.

The importance of music education in Portugal, with its deep roots in the nation's rich history of artistic expression and its vital role in cultivating a deeper appreciation for the captivating sounds of the Iberian nation, has become a cornerstone of the country's broader educational system, serving as a means of nurturing the next generation of musicians, composers, and cultural ambassadors. Through the dedicated efforts of educators who have committed themselves to the task of preserving and perpetuating the enduring power of Portuguese music, the collective identity and artistic sensibilities of the Portuguese people have been indelibly shaped, ensuring that this captivating art form will continue to resonate with audiences both within and beyond the borders of the Iberian Peninsula.

Alongside the remarkable efforts to promote and cultivate music education in Portugal, the tireless work of cultural preservationists has emerged as a vital complement to these endeavors, serving as the guardians of the nation's distinctive musical instruments and the captivating traditional music forms that have long defined the Iberian nation's artistic heritage. From the iconic Portuguese guitar to the regional folk instruments that have become the sonic signatures of local communities, these remarkable tools of musical expression have been safeguarded and restored through the meticulous efforts of skilled luthiers and dedicated community advocates, ensuring that the enduring power and resonance of these captivating cultural legacies will continue to be experienced by audiences for generations to come.

Moreover, the symbiotic relationship between music education and preservation efforts in Portugal has become increasingly apparent, as these two vital components of the nation's cultural heritage have worked in close collaboration to cultivate a deeper understanding and appreciation for the enduring power of the Iberian nation's musical traditions. Through the incorporation of specialized knowledge, performance techniques, and historical contexts into the curricula of music education institutions, the remarkable preservation efforts that have emerged to safeguard Portugal's traditional music and instruments have played a crucial role in shaping the next generation of musicians, composers, and cultural ambassadors who will be tasked with the ongoing responsibility of perpetuating this precious artistic legacy.

As the world continues to grapple with the challenges of globalization and the homogenization of cultural traditions, the remarkable efforts to promote music education and preservation in Portugal have become increasingly crucial, serving as a vital bulwark against the erosion of the nation's artistic heritage and a powerful means of cultivating a deeper appreciation for the enduring power of musical expression. Through the tireless work of dedicated educators, cultural preservationists, and community advocates, the captivating sounds of Portuguese music will continue to resonate with audiences both within and beyond the borders of the Iberian Peninsula, serving as a vital reflection of the nation's collective identity and a testament to the remarkable resilience and adaptability of its cultural legacy.

DISCLAIMER

The publisher and the author are providing this book and its contents on an "as is" basis and make no representations or warranties of any kind concerning this book or its contents. This is a work of nonfiction. No names have been changed, no characters invented, and no events fabricated.

Although the publisher and the author have made every effort to ensure that the information in this book was correct at press time and while this publication is designed to provide accurate information regarding the subject matter covered, the publisher and the author assume no responsibility for mistakes, inaccuracies, omissions, or any other inconsistencies herein and hereby disclaim any liability to any party for any loss, damage, or disruption caused by mistakes or omissions, whether such mistakes or omissions result from negligence, accident, or any other cause.

ABOUT THE AUTHOR

Maher Asaad Baker (In Arabic: ماهر أسعد بكر), is a Syrian musician, author, journalist, VFX & graphic artist, and director. He was born in Damascus in 1977. He grew up with a dream of being one of the most well-known artists in the world, and he has been working hard to achieve it ever since.

He started his career in 1997 when he was only 20 years old. He had a passion for technology and media, and he taught himself how to develop applications and websites. He also explored various types of media-creating paths, such as music production, graphic design, video editing, animation, and filmmaking. He was not satisfied with just being a consumer of media; he wanted to be a creator of media.

Reading was another source of inspiration for him. He was always surrounded by books as a child, thanks to his father's extensive library. He read books from different genres, topics, and perspectives. He read books for knowledge, for wisdom, for entertainment, for enlightenment. Reading stimulated his imagination and curiosity. Reading also developed his writing skills.

He did not start writing professionally until later in his life, as he was busy with other projects and pursuits. But when he did start writing, he proved himself to be a talented and prolific writer. He wrote articles for various newspapers and magazines on topics such as politics, culture, society, art, technology, and more. He wrote books that were informative and insightful. He wrote books that were creative and captivating. He wrote books that were best-selling and award-winning.

He is most known for his book "How I wrote a million Wikipedia articles", where he shares his experience of being one of the most prolific contributors to the online encyclopedia. He reveals his methods, techniques, strategies, and secrets of writing high-quality articles on any subject in record time. He also discusses the benefits and challenges of being a Wikipedia editor in the age of information overload.

He is also known for his novel "Becoming the man", where he tells the story of a young man who goes through a series of transformations in his life. The novel explores themes such as identity, masculinity, self-discovery, love, loss, and redemption. The novel is based on his journey to becoming who he is today.

Copyright © 2024 Maher Asaad Baker

All rights reserved. No part of this document may be reproduced or transmitted in any form or by any means, electronic, mechanical, photocopying, recording, or otherwise, without prior written permission of the publisher.
